SOUTH
SOUTH
NAMIBIA • BOTSWANA •

Martin Gostelow
Bernard Joliat

JPMGUIDES

skilled artisans

CONTENTS

wine lands

nature in the wild

rainbow nation

THIS WAY SOUTH AFRICA

With as many facets as a kaleidoscope, the land now called the Republic of South Africa has been attracting Europeans since the second half of the 17th century. Its strategic importance, fertile soils, enviable climate, fabulous mineral riches and unparalleled natural attractions have long been irresistible lures.

At the tip of the African continent, between the Atlantic and Indian oceans, South Africa has a varied landscape. The craggy mountains of the uKhahlamba-Drakensberg could hardly be more different from the red plains of the Kalahari, the forests and lakes of the Garden Route, or the acacia bush of the Kruger Park. Molten gold being poured in the mines of bustling Johannesburg provides a striking counterpoint to the Stone Age rock art, traditional Zulu villages and sleepy settler towns studded with Cape Dutch buildings found elsewhere in the country.

For years, the political policies of the apartheid era ensured that the majority of potential international visitors shunned South Africa. All that has changed since 1994, when the first democratic election was held: today, South Africa is the most popular tourist destination on the continent.

Towns, Flowers, Vineyards
A busy commercial city, Johannesburg offers the sort of sights you might expect in Manhattan. In its pagan temples of concrete and smoked glass, the sacred rites are centred on the fluctuating prices of gold, platinum, uranium and diamonds. Looking out over its sprawling suburbs as your plane comes in to land, you might find it difficult to believe that Johannesburg, founded in 1886, will only be 125 years old in 2011.

The region around Pretoria—called Jacaranda City for its avenues of trees that blossom into purple clouds in October—is scattered with mansions and monuments that encapsulate in stone and bronze the country's exciting history.

Cape Town, beautifully sited beneath Table Mountain, forms with the Cape Peninsula a floral kingdom. South of the city,

Kirstenbosch Botanical Gardens displays many of the 18,000 flower species found within the Republic.

Travelling inland from Cape Town, you pass through some of the lushest land on earth. The vineyards of Stellenbosch, Paarl and Franschhoek produce some of South Africa's best-known wines. Travellers who choose to follow the Garden Route along the south coast can make stops at a dozen beach resorts as well as stopping to take a look at industrial Port Elizabeth and East London—not forgetting the inland detour to the ostrich farms of Oudtshoorn.

Flanked by extensive beaches of fine sand, Durban, with its sophisticated lifestyle and facilities for water sports, makes a splendid starting point or finale to a tour along the Indian Ocean shores. To the west stand the towers and crags of uKhahlamba-Drakensberg, a mountain wall to be crossed before you reach the rolling farmlands of the Free State.

Fascinating Cultures
Wearing headdresses made from buffalo horn, their bodies daubed with war paint and hung with tribal ornaments, the descendants of the mighty *impis* (armies) of Shaka Zulu wait in ambush, leaping suddenly out of the Zululand

A geography lesson. Covering more than five times the area of the British Isles, South Africa is a melting pot of the human race. Inhabiting a territory of 1,219,000 sq km (470,000 sq miles), the population of almost 50 million is made up of 79% black Africans, 9.6% whites, 8.9% coloured and 2.5% Indians and Asians. Together they are endeavouring to build one of the richest countries on earth.

landscape to catch visitors unawares. Such historically evocative encounters—friendly nowadays—provides much needed employment for the actors, and are a delight for the photographer.

Other cultures also enjoy the opportunity to explain their traditions and astonish visitors with their rites, costumes, colours and art. The most surprising of these are the Ndebele, a minority community in the Pretoria region. Long before western Cubists dreamed up the idea, Ndebele artists were practising this type of painting, covering the walls of their dwellings in radiant colours and bold geometrical patterns.

Safari Country
South Africa is the domain of the wild animal—close encounters are virtually guaranteed. Hluh-

luwe-iMfolozi, Mala Mala, Londolozi and Sabi Sabi, among many other national and private game reserves, offer you the privilege of seeing the great beasts in their own environment — rhinoceros, elephant, hippopotamus, lion, leopard, cheetah, buffalo, giraffe, antelope and zebra are all here. However, none of these reserves can compare in scale or variety with the Kruger National Park, South Africa's greatest animal sanctuary.

Where to Stay

You'll be pleasantly surprised by the high standards of accommodation. At the top end of the scale, five-star hotels are most prolific in the Cape Town area and the prosperous suburbs of Johannesburg, but they can also be found at most other major attractions. The coastal resorts near Durban and along the Garden Route have hotels for every budget. Along the well-trodden holiday routes, in the uKhahlamba-Drakensberg mountains, the Northern and Western Cape, Mpumalanga, Limpopo Province and the Free State, country-house hotels and family homes offer bed and breakfast. In the game parks, the options range from chalet self-catering and hotels near the major park entrances to the ultimate in luxury at one of the private lodges.

South African Tourism

The King Protea *(Protea cynaroides)* is South Africa's national flower.

Listen to the Sunrise

In South Africa, everything is possible. Can you imagine the atmosphere of a Mzumba traditional dance, where a hundred drums beat in rhythm and a thousand feet hammer the ground? Have you ever heard the jackal's love call, or stopped to listen to the sounds of sunrise or dusk over the African bush?

One thing is certain: however long your stay in this country, it won't be long enough to sample the countless attractions.

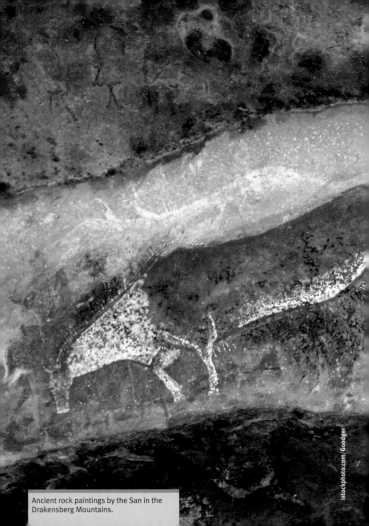

Ancient rock paintings by the San in the Drakensberg Mountains.

FLASHBACK

Africa is the cradle of humanity. The East African Rift Valley has yielded fossils that represent practically every stage in hominid evolution. South Africa's oldest-known hominid fossil skull, discovered in the Sterkfontein Caves (now part of the Cradle of Humankind World Heritage Site west of Johannesburg), is around 2.5 million years old.

Southern Africa's earliest inhabitants were hunter-gatherers. This lifestyle was still practised in arid and mountainous parts of the region by the San (or Bushmen) in the 15th century, when Europeans first landed at the Cape. In more moist areas, hunter-gatherers had been all but supplanted by pastoralists such as the Khoikhoi (or Hottentots) of the southern Cape and the Bantu-speaking people of the eastern coastline and interior.

The First Europeans
In 1485, with the arrival of Diego Cão, the Portuguese became the first recorded Europeans to set foot on the soil of southern Africa. The following year, on December 8, 1486, Bartolomeu Dias landed at the place now known as Mossel Bay. A few weeks later he discovered the site of the future Cape Town. Ten years on, Vasco da Gama sailed from the bay of Saint Helena to the KwaZulu-Natal coast. He was the first man in history to round the Cape of Good Hope and open the route to India for western navigators.

Early Settlers
The "European" history of South Africa had begun, but no one thought of settling in the region until 1652. Commanding three ships and some hundred men, Jan Van Riebeeck established a strategic revictualling point at the Cape for the ships of the Dutch East India Company. Five years later the first colonists had arrived, and in 1685, 200 Huguenots, French Protestant refugees, landed near the Cape, where they soon integrated with the established Dutch community. They also had the foresight to introduce the cultivation of vines. Dutch,

French and, later, German settlers gradually merged to become the people now referred to as Afrikaners, and communicated in a Dutch-based language called Afrikaans.

Next to settle were Malays and Malagasy, brought in by the Dutch East India Company as labourers. Some colonists who found it hard to bear the constraints imposed by the Company became semi-nomadic pastoral farmers known as the *trekboeren*. Weakened by smallpox and other diseases, the Khoikhoi were unable to resist this expansion. Some intermarried with others of the Cape population and their descendants now form part of the mixed race Cape Coloured community.

The indigenous Bantu-speaking people, such as the Zulu of KwaZulu-Natal and the Xhosa of the Eastern Cape, provided stauncher resistance to European settlement, starting with the Xhosa frontier wars of 1779 onwards. Prosperity

The Cape began to prosper, largely through trade with the trekboeren who bartered their cattle for arms, coffee and sugar. Rivalry between England and France (which was allied with the Dutch), both in the Americas and in Europe, had its repercussions in South Africa. The British, who wanted to control the route to the Indies, captured the Cape in 1795 but returned it to the Batavian Republic, as the Dutch government was then called, under the Treaty of Amiens in 1802. (By that time the Dutch East Indian Company was extinct.) But the eastern districts were in turmoil, and with the resumption of the Napoleonic Wars, the British recaptured the Cape from Napoleon's Dutch allies in 1806. Their title was confirmed in 1814 by the Treaty of Paris.

The British Arrive

British colonization did not begin in earnest until 1820, with the arrival of 5000 settlers in what is today the Eastern Cape. With them they brought notions of freedom of the press, civil rights and humanitarian ideals. They established Anglican missions and English as the official language. In 1828 the Khoikhoi and Cape Coloured people were given freedom of movement; slavery was abolished in 1834. The emancipated slaves and the Khoikhoi became a rural and urban working class. All these measures were unacceptable to the Boers, who were also forced to return to indigenous peoples land acquired in the frontier wars of 1834–35.

The Boers Leave

Many Afrikaners came to the conclusion that they could not

live as they wished under British rule. Between 1835 and 1843, some 12,000 of them, together with their cattle, sheep and wagons, set out, Bible in hand, on the Great Trek. Some settled by the Orange River, others continued northwards to the Limpopo and the future Transvaal, the remainder travelled eastwards across the uKhahlamba-Drakensberg and into KwaZulu-Natal. This land was occupied by Sotho, Ndebele, Zulu and other indigenous Bantu-speakers, who resisted Boer settlement. A series of altercations culminated in the Battle of Blood River, wherein a small Boer laager, led by Andries Pretorius (namesake of Pretoria) and armed with muskets, laid waste to the spear-wielding Zulu army in 1838.

British-Boer Rivalry

The trekkers founded two new republics based on strict, puritanical Calvinism: the Transvaal in 1852 and the Orange Free State in 1854. South Africa was thus divided into two Afrikaner republics and two relatively liberal British colonies, neither of which gave much legal recognition to indigenous Africans.

With the intention of unifying the four white states of southern Africa (the Cape, Natal, Orange Free State and the Transvaal), the British annexed the Transvaal in 1877. They then moved to eliminate the danger presented by the Zulus' military strength. Under their chief Cetshwayo, the Zulus routed a large British force at Isandlwana in 1879 but were conquered the following year at Ulundi. The Transvaal Afrikaners, who had initially accepted annexation, eventually put up a formidable resistance led by Paul Kruger, Marthinus Pretorius (son of Andries) and Piet Joubert. The struggle ended with the defeat of a British force at Majuba Hill in 1881. The Transvaal thereby gained full internal autonomy.

Gold and Diamonds

The discovery of diamonds at Kimberley in 1867 and of the Witwatersrand goldfields in 1886 attracted a tidal wave of prospectors and opportunists, mostly British. In the Transvaal, Kruger denied these Uitlanders (foreigners) civil rights, but they continued to pour in. By 1896 they outnumbered the Boers seven to one.

Meanwhile, in the Cape, Cecil Rhodes, diamond magnate and controller of De Beers, had appeared on the scene. As prime minister he formed an alliance with the Afrikaner Hofmeyr which held the hope of healing the Anglo-Afrikaner rift and of building good relations between whites and non-whites in the Cape colony. But as the European

istockphoto.com/Walker

It all started with the discovery of a diamond in 1867, and thousands rushed to the Kimberley.

race to colonize Africa accelerated, Rhodes began annexing territory surrounding the Afrikaner republics and making plans for a British South African federation.

Frustrated by Kruger, Rhodes plotted his overthrow. At the end of 1895, one of his supporters, Dr Jameson, led a raid into the Transvaal, ostensibly to "save" the Uitlanders from persecution. But they failed to rise as Jameson had hoped. He was forced to surrender, and Rhodes resigned as prime minister. When the British presented Kruger with an ultimatum on the Uitlanders' franchise, war was inevitable. Kruger remained unmoved, and in 1899 the second Anglo-Boer war broke out.

The Boer War

Although they sympathized with Kruger's cause, the Boer community in the Cape did not rise up but offered only moral support. Both sides paid a heavy price in a war that was to last three years. At first the Boers held the British forces at bay at the Tugela in Natal for almost a year while laying siege to Ladysmith, Mafeking (now Mahikeng) and Kimberley. Once the British had broken through at Tugela and invaded the Orange Free State, the Boers began to use guerrilla tactics against their columns. By 1902, the British were burning Boer farms and interning civilians in camps where more than 20,000 died—the first "concentration camps". The Boers appealed for help, and many volunteers responded—Irish, American, even Russian—seeing the anti-colonialist cause as their own. But any hopes of support from the governments of Germany, France and the Netherlands were dashed. Britain called on its generals, Roberts and Kitchener, together with troops from Australia, New Zealand and Canada, as well as

100,000 black and Cape Coloured auxiliaries. The Boers were eventually forced to surrender. Kruger signed the Treaty of Vereeniging in the Transvaal on May 31, 1902. The British were left in charge of the goldfields, but their losses totalled more than 25,000 men.

The Start of Segregation
Amnesty was granted to the rebels, along with freedom for prisoners, recognition of the Afrikaner language and financial help with reconstruction. Four years later, the two erstwhile warring communities came together to suppress the revolt of the Zulus of Natal. The Union of South Africa was declared on May 31, 1910, with the Boer General Louis Botha as Prime Minister. This was two years before the foundation of the African National Congress (ANC) which aspired to persuade the white community to accord blacks full political rights. It proved to be a vain hope, and in 1913 the Native Land Act prevented Africans from acquiring land outside the reserves.

With the Allies
The economic crisis of 1929 and the outbreak of World War II in 1939 accentuated the division between the English and Afrikaner communities. Pro-German in the great European conflict, the Afrikaners tried to keep their country neutral. But prime minister Jan Smuts, who had little sympathy with Nazi ideals, brought South Africa into the war on the side of the Allies. Nevertheless, South Africa's Ossewabrandwag, a party of 400,000 Nazi enthusiasts, openly supported Hitler.

Farewell to the Commonwealth
Protests and strikes by the black trade unions from 1940 onwards met with repression, especially after the election, in 1948, of an ultra-right-wing Nationalist government under D.F. Malan. In 1950, mixed marriages or even sexual relations between black and white were prohibited, as well as any political party or association opposed to apartheid (the Afrikaans word for "separateness"). In 1952, the work permit became obligatory for black Africans, and the passbook was required for any travelling. A demonstration at Sharpeville on March 21, 1960 by the ANC movement was fired on by security forces, killing 61 blacks. The ANC, directed first by Albert Luthuli (Nobel laureate for peace in 1960) and later by Nelson Mandela, was outlawed. Following a referendum, the Union of South Africa withdrew from the Commonwealth and became the Republic of South Africa.

Setback

The politics of apartheid were pursued despite general worldwide condemnation. To limit the danger threatened by the overcrowded townships, some of the black population was moved out to "homelands", conceived to encourage "separate development". In this way the artificial states of Transkei, Ciskei, Bophuthatswana and Venda were created, though they were refused recognition by the UN. Excluded from international sport and the object of commercial boycotts, South Africa suffered more and more from its isolation.

Revolution

A new law that obliged all schools to use the Afrikaans language in their teaching provoked the Soweto riots of 1976. The incidents marked the beginning of an undercover revolution. P.W. Botha, elected President in 1978, tried in vain to save apartheid by easing its laws superficially, largely under pressure from local financial interests who were concerned by the export of capital. The Constitution of 1983 tried to increase the power of the Indian and Coloured populations. In 1986 the laws against mixed marriages and interracial relations were dropped, the passbook was suppressed, and certain facilities were granted to black leaders.

The Search for Peace

Desmond Tutu, the Anglican archbishop of Cape Town, exerted his influence to achieve better understanding and mutual respect between the opposing groups; he received the 1984 Nobel Peace Prize for his efforts. However, the violence continued with the support of the ANC, whose leaders, including Nelson Mandela, had been arrested and condemned to life imprisonment in 1964. Those who escaped arrest were forced into exile. A state of emergency was declared in 1985 and continued until 1990.

The End of Apartheid

In 1989, F.W. de Klerk was elected by the National Party to succeed P.W. Botha. At his investiture, de Klerk promised freedom to all political prisoners and lifted the ban on the ANC and other dissident groups. He later released Nelson Mandela, who had spent 27 years behind bars. Mandela and de Klerk then entered into tentative negotiations to replace apartheid with a more egalitarian system of government.

At the end of 1991, the Convention for Democratic South Africa (Codesa) was created by 17 parties, who established the basis for a new united South Africa free of racial discrimination. Only the extreme left and the extreme right abstained.

The Triumph of Reason

In a referendum held the following year, 68 per cent of the white population accepted the movement towards reform. The first multiracial elections were programmed for 1994. The UN lifted its economic sanctions, de Klerk and Mandela jointly received the Nobel Peace Prize, and South Africa rejoined the Commonwealth.

The new Cape Town stadium near the Victoria & Alfred waterfront was built for the World Cup 2010.

Modern Times

Multi-racial classes started the school year in 1994. On Sunday, April 24, 1994, long queues of people of all races and all cultures formed in front of the polling stations to exercise their right to vote. To general surprise and relief, the elections passed off peacefully. The ANC won by a convincing majority and Nelson Mandela was elected State President. Due largely to his wisdom, the country's peaceful transition to a majority rule was a political miracle.

Thabo Mbeki succeeded Mandela as president in 1999 and was re-elected in 2004. From then until 2008, the government was tainted by infighting between Mbeki and his former deputy Jacob Zuma, who was sacked by Mbeki due to his involvement in corruption charges. Nevertheless, Zuma was elected as ANC president in 2008, causing Mbeki to resign in September 2008. Kgalema Motlanthe was appointed as caretaker president in Mbeki's stead and held the position until May 2009, when the ANC was returned to power in a general election and Zuma took over as state president.

Today the ANC is confronted by a host of problems, some inherited from the former administration, others of its own creation. These include housing shortages, mass unemployment, high crime levels, the world's largest number of HIV/Aids infected people, and a culture of corruption that permeates every tier of local and national government. While the ANC enjoyed mixed success in tackling these problems, the mood in the country remains positive, and it was buoyed greatly by its successful hosting of the FIFA World Cup in June/July 2010.

NELSON MANDELA

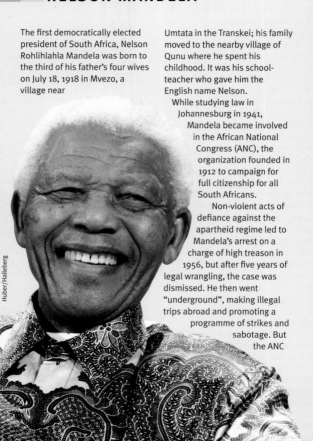

The first democratically elected president of South Africa, Nelson Rohlihlahla Mandela was born to the third of his father's four wives on July 18, 1918 in Mvezo, a village near Umtata in the Transkei; his family moved to the nearby village of Qunu where he spent his childhood. It was his school-teacher who gave him the English name Nelson.

While studying law in Johannesburg in 1941, Mandela became involved in the African National Congress (ANC), the organization founded in 1912 to campaign for full citizenship for all South Africans.

Non-violent acts of defiance against the apartheid regime led to Mandela's arrest on a charge of high treason in 1956, but after five years of legal wrangling, the case was dismissed. He then went "underground", making illegal trips abroad and promoting a programme of strikes and sabotage. But the ANC

Huber/Halleberg

was ill-prepared for this role. It had been penetrated by the state security forces and in August 1962 Mandela was arrested again and sentenced first to five years, and then to life imprisonment.

Robben Island became his home for 18 years. In winter rain and summer heat, the convicts chipped the white rock in its quarry; Mandela's eyesight was damaged by the dazzling reflection and dust. As the lowest class of prisoner, he was allowed one visitor and one letter every six months. But the world had not forgotten. When apartheid at last began to crumble, there was no alternative open to the government but to talk to him. He was moved to the mainland, then to a hospital, and finally released on February 11, 1990. In 1993 he and de Klerk were jointly awarded the Nobel Peace Prize. A year later, he led the ANC to victory in the country's first fully democratic elections and became the first black to govern South Africa. Now in his 90s and retired from public life, Mandela is still revered at home and abroad for moral authority and astonishing degree of forgiveness that held the nation together during the 1994 elections and in challenging years that followed.

Huber/Huw

Johannesburg is a modern commercial city, with memories of the past ever present.

ON THE SCENE

South Africa is a mosaic of ethnic groups and landscapes, of cultures and traditions, of wild beasts and rare plants. Each of its provinces covers an immense area offering constant variety and a wide diversity of natural and cultural sites. It is impossible to see everything in one trip, but why worry? After all, you will surely want to come back to this land of adventure. This book follows the division of South Africa into nine modern provinces: Gauteng, Limpopo, Northwest, Mpumalanga, Free State, KwaZulu-Natal, Eastern Cape, Northern Cape and Western Cape.

Gauteng

Gauteng—"place of gold" in the Sotho language—was delineated as recently as 1994, when the country's four established provinces (whose borders conformed to those of the pre-Union Cape and Natal Colonies and Transvaal and Free State Boer Republics) were divided into nine smaller ones. Consisting of Pretoria, the Witwatersrand, Johannesburg and Vereeniging, Gauteng is by far the smallest of South Africa's new provinces, accounting for about 1.4 per cent of the country's surface area, but it is also the most urbanized and densely populated part of the country, supporting approximately 10 million people.

With direct flights from many foreign cities, O.R. Tambo International Airport, east of Johannesburg and south of Pretoria, is the main gateway to South Africa. Most visitors use Gauteng as little more than an overnight stop and a springboard for their travels to more scenic parts of the country.

Johannesburg

Situated on a plateau at an altitude of 1,800 m (5,900 ft), Johannesburg is Southern Africa's commercial and economic metropolis, and the focal point of what is certainly the largest urban conglomeration in Africa. Yet, by the standards of European cities, Johannesburg is barely out of its infancy, founded on an otherwise

Hand-made *djembe* on sale at an open-air market.

istockphoto.com/Parnell

grid-iron street pattern broken only by **Diagonal Street**, a metaphor for the stock exchange, whose building used to stand beside it. Erected in 1983, the nearby **Anglo-American Building** has the form of a diamond whose facets reflect the colours of the sky. Elsewhere, above a busy African street scene, tall modern office buildings that were abandoned in the flight to safer and pleasanter suburbs in the 1990s are now mostly reoccupied, emblematic of the city's recent urban renewal.

Some unusual souvenirs can be found in the shops of *sangomas* (traditional healers), among them magic potions, fetishes and statuettes, along with a fine selection of aphrodisiacs. Asian shopkeepers have a wide variety of Indian goods on sale at **Oriental Plaza**, further west in the Newtown area.

unremarkable tract of grassland in 1886, when one George Harrison found a huge nugget of gold and triggered off a rush that attracted thousands of hopeful prospectors. The boomtown of Johannesburg, which fell to the British at the end of the Boer War (1899–1902), grew to become one of the great cities of the world.

City Centre
Experiencing something of a resurrection after years of stagnation, central Johannesburg has a

Market Theatre
Northwest of Diagonal Street, some of South Africa's best actors are to be seen performing in the three theatres of the Market Theatre complex. There are also two art galleries, a restaurant, a bar and a shopping area, not to mention a flea market every weekend—in short, something for everyone.

The **Museum Africa** nearby in Bree Street has a remarkable collection of Stone Age Bushman paintings.

Hillbrow

North of the city centre near Hillbrow Hospital, the **Adler Museum of Medicine and Dentistry** is one of Johannesburg's more disconcerting museums. The 40,000 items collected here include 19th-century medical instruments, a curious African herbarium, and the medical bag of an African sangoma. A display is devoted to Professor Christiaan Barnard, who carried out the world's first heart transplant in 1969.

Traditionally cosmopolitan, Hillbrow is today a focal point for legal and illegal migrants from elsewhere in Africa, as well as having the unenviable reputation of being the single biggest crime hotspot in the country. Peppered with night clubs and restaurants, most of them decidedly disreputable, Hillbrow is—wisely—avoided by most tourists.

Built in 1896 in Tudor style, the **Windybrow Theatre** served as a homestead and later a nurses' home before becoming an arts centre in the 1980s. It stages plays by African writers.

Ellis Park

At Doornfontein, 3 km (almost 2 miles) east of the city centre, Ellis Park attracts crowds of avid rugby and football fans. With a bit of luck, visitors may be able to watch a top-level international or domestic match. This is the stadium where South Africa's Springboks won the world rugby championship in 1995, with President Nelson Mandela proudly cheering them on (as immortalized in the 2009 film *Invictus*). It was also the setting for five matches in the 2010 FIFA World Cup, including the quarter-final between Paraguay and the eventual champions Spain.

Gold Reef City

The mining town of Gold Reef City has become Johannesburg's principal tourist attraction. The headgear of Crown Mines No. 14 shaft marks the site of what was once the world's deepest mine, at 3,200 m (10,500 ft), employing 30,000 miners. It closed in 1977 and has been transformed into a vast theme park and open-air museum. Accurate historical reconstructions transport visitors back in time to the 1880s and the early days of the Gold Rush. A lift takes you down an old mine shaft to a depth of 220 m (720 ft). Above ground, the saloons, banks and shops of the era recreate the old-time atmosphere.

Apartheid Museum

Next to the casino, this well-designed museum documents the rise and fall of apartheid and shows, in an emotional journey through the past, how the country is working towards a better future.

Northern Suburbs

Since the year 2000, big business and upmarket commercial interests (including most tourist facilities) have generally migrated from the city centre to the leafy northern suburbs. The prestigious suburb of **Sandton** is the site of the largest concentration of tourist hotels around Johannesburg, as well as several large shopping malls.

Also serviced by several classy hotels and shops, **Rosebank** is of interest for its Rooftop Market, an excellent place to go craft shopping. By contrast, the trendy suburb of **Melville** is studded with lively street cafés, live music venues, arty shops and restaurants.

Soweto

From 1945 onwards, the number of black South Africans drawn to work in Johannesburg greatly increased. At first, informal settlements developed to meet the lack of housing then, with the implementation of apartheid, townships were created outside legally designated white areas, to accommodate migrant workers evicted from the inner city.

In 1963, the sprawling township was officially named Soweto (an acronym of South Western Township). Its endless rows of identical single-storey houses were built on one level to facilitate police intervention and the disbanding of anti-apartheid political groups. Unfortunately, the housing provided did little to improve the lot of the blacks. Almost 2 million people live in this township today.

Pretoria (Tshwane)

An hour's drive from Johannesburg, the political capital Pretoria

Soweto sights. From Johannesburg or Pretoria, private operators will take you on a tour of South Africa's most famous township. Small groups of visitors are guided by formidable local ladies, who point out the locations that made the news during the anti-apartheid campaigns: Regina Mundi Church, focus of protest rallies; Archbishop Tutu's house; the the Hector Pieterson Museum (named for a student shot dead by the police; the Mandela house, long disputed between supporters of Nelson Mandela and his estranged ex-wife Winnie and now the unprepossessing Mandela Family Museum; the shebeens (beer halls); markets selling anything from CDs to tribal medicines; and "Millionaires' Row", grand houses built for successful black entrepreneurs when they had no choice as to where to live. On the edges of Soweto, thousands of minibuses (mainly unlicensed) gather to transport its residents to their jobs in Johannesburg.

is now part of Tshwane Municipality. Pretoria is not as exciting as Johannesburg, but it boasts a wider range of historical attractions and is arguably less crime-ridden. It is named after Andries Pretorius, the Boer general who defeated the Zulu army at Blood River in 1838 and whose son later became president of the Transvaal.

Pretoria is today a peaceful administrative centre and university city. It became the capital of the Boer Republic of Transvaal in 1855. Its development accelerated with the gold rush of 1886, followed by the diamond rush at Cullinan, situated only 20 km (12.5 miles) away to the east.

In Kruger's Footsteps
Pretoria is linked to the history of Paul Kruger, last president of Transvaal, who was born in 1825 in the Cape Colony, participated in the Great Trek at age 10, and died in exile in Switzerland in 1904. His home in Church Street has been turned into the **Kruger House Museum** displaying furniture and objects which belonged to the legendary statesman, as well as mementoes of the Boer War.

In **Church Square**, to the east, stands a statue of Kruger by Anton van Wouw. In the southwest corner of the square, the Council Chamber was the seat of the old Boer Republic.

hemis.fr/Maisant

A monument to Paul Kruger in Church Square, Pretoria.

State Theatre
To the east of Church Square, the State Theatre is home to a magnificent artistic complex of six auditoria. Guided tours are available. This temple devoted to the arts is used not only for operatic, dramatic and choral productions, but also for ballet performances and symphony concerts. Try to visit on Saturdays when a lively flea market buzzes outside.

City Hall
Further south, the old City Hall stands out on Paul Kruger Ave-

nue. It is a splendid piece of Victorian grandeur: the clock tower has a peal of 32 bells accompanied by an organ of 6,800 pipes. Statues of Andries Pretorius, the pioneer general, and his son Marthinus, the president, stand in front of the building.

The **Transvaal Museum of Natural History**, opposite, is one of the best in South Africa, with displays of mammals and other species, exhibits relating to early man, and the definitive collection of stuffed South African birds.

To see living examples, visit the **National Zoological Gardens**, in a 600 ha (1,500-acre) park just north of the centre.

Union Buildings

In the centre of a park laid out with handsome gardens, the red sandstone Union Buildings (1913) designed by Sir Herbert Baker are the administrative seat of government and home to the National Archives. In 1994 this was the scene of the investiture of President Nelson Mandela before 42 heads of state and 5,000 other foreign dignitaries.

Voortrekker Monument

Even this event failed to totter the Voortrekker Monument, on a hilltop south of the city. This imposing granite edifice symbolizes the era of the Great Trek (1835–38) and the intransigence of the Boers in their fight for independence. Inside is the domed Hall of Heroes with a marble historical frieze. The circular outer granite wall is carved with 64 ox-wagons representing the famed *laager* of the Voortrekkers. The nearby Fort Schanskop is now a museum of Voortrekker life.

Cullinan

Some 50 minutes by road east of Pretoria, the fabled Cullinan diamond mine is still in operation. The vertical pipe of heavy blue diamond-bearing rock at the Premier mine is the oldest deposit of kimberlite known to exist—a trifling 1,700 million years old. One quarter of all stones worldwide of more than 400 carats uncut weight have come from this mine. This is where the Star of Africa and other gigantic gems originated.

Visits are closely supervised. Although you will not be encouraged to help yourself to a few kimberlite souvenirs, it is possible to buy some small pieces at the mine shop—said to contain minute diamonds, sometimes.

Mapoch Cultural Village

Northeast of Pretoria, near Hammanskraal, the brightly painted village of Mapoch offers a unique opportunity to see something of the local Ndebele people's traditional way of life.

Famous for their uniquely styled house paintings, the Ndebele artists are clearly fond of the straight line, even if the occasional circle does creep into the dazzling display of superimposed diagonals, squares and rectangles in bright colours edged in black, on a white background. House-painting is essentially a female occupation; the men have drearier work down the nearby mines. The painters express their talent on the outside walls of their dwellings, while craftswomen use the same designs to create jewellery, blankets and clothing, which have even inspired dress designers of Cape Town and Johannesburg. Married women wear bronze rings around their arms, necks and ankles, though these tend to be replaced nowadays by thick coils made up of thousands of glass beads strung onto wire.

Mapoch is part of the open-air **Tswaing Museum**, whose centrepiece is the Tswaing Crater, 1 km wide and 100 m deep, which was created by meteor impact some 250,000 years ago. It has a pretty lake at its centre. A walking trail runs through the crater, which is tentatively listed as a potential UNESCO World Heritage Site.

In paint or in beads, traditional Ndebele designs are solid blocks of colour outlined in black.

The extraordinary architecture of Sun City includes concrete elephants.

Northwest

Northwest is a thinly populated farming and mining region is best known for the glitzy Sun City and the wilder Pilanesberg and Madikwe game reserves. At Mahikeng there are still reminders of the Boer War, where British defenders led by Baden-Powell were besieged for 217 days.

Sun City

The somewhat surreal "Lost City", 150 km (94 miles) from Johannesburg, was designed by Sol Kerzner to provide white South Africans with a local version of Las Vegas and the chance to wallow in conspicuous consumption. Just two hours by hotel courtesy bus from O.R. Tambo International Airport, Sun City is devoted entirely to pleasure. People come from the world over to play in the casinos, see the shows and, when sated with man-made entertainment, go on safari to commune with nature.

Pilanesberg Game Reserve

This tract of wooded savannah centred on Lake Mankwe is home to abundant wildlife—including reintroduced lion, elephant and rhino—and guarantees an unforgettable photo safari. Located on the verge of the Kalahari biome, Pilanesberg supports numerous western bird species at the eastern extent of their range, notably the stunning (and vocal) crimson-breasted shrike—a good selection can be seen in the walk-in aviary at the main entrance gate. Birds and mammals are most active in the early morning, so it's worth staying in a chalet or tent within the reserve, which is dotted with strange rock formations of volcanic origin. Guided night drives offer a good chance of seeing shy creatures such as brown hyena, aardwolf and genet.

Madikwe Game Reserve

Established along the Botswana border in 1991, the 750 sq km Madikwe Game Reserve has emerged as an increasingly popular alternative to the Kruger Park, partly due to the total absence of malaria. The reserve protects an open tract of dry woodland and savannah that runs north from the base of the Dwarsberg Mountains. Plenty of game occurs there naturally, and more than 8,000 animals were translocated there in the 1990s. The reserve is serviced by a handful of small private lodges, most of which offer similar all-inclusive packages (including game drives and guided walks) to the private reserves bordering Kruger, but at lower cost. In addition to the Big Five, Madikwe harbours cheetah, African wild dog, spotted hyena, giraffe, zebra, various antelope and a diversity of dry-country birds.

istockphoto.com/Martins

Limpopo Province

Limpopo (formerly Northern) Province, named after the river that runs along its northern border with Zimbabwe and Botswana, is steeped in history: ruins and remains emerge from dense forest intersected by waterfalls and torrents rich in trout. Tea plantations and vast orchards complement the sub-tropical vegetation.

Polokwane

The first town you meet on the long N1 highway from Pretoria is **Bela-Bela** (formerly Warmbaths), known for its hot springs. But there are still another hundred or so kilometres to go before you reach Polokwane (formerly Pietersburg), an agricultural centre and the biggest town of the region, founded in 1886. In the **Bakone Malapa Open-Air Museum**, 9 km (6 miles) outside town, you can visit a *kraal*, or traditional village, and learn something of the way of life of the northern Sothos.

Louis Trichardt

If you follow the N1 north towards Zimbabwe, you will reach

istockphoto.com/Gallas

Huber/Simeone

Traditional Venda dress; the Venda homeland is centred on Thohoyandou near the Zimbabwe border. | **The baobab stores water in its trunk.** | **Tea plantations near Tzaneen.**

the historic town of Louis Trichardt, after one of the most famous Voortrekkers. In 2003 the name was changed to Makhado and the statue of Trichardt replaced by that of the Venda King Makhado, but the decision was reversed by the Supreme Court Appeal in 2007. South of the town, the **Ben Lavin Nature Reserve** is home to numerous species of animals and birds.

To the northwest, the **Soutpansberg trail** crosses a forested range of mountains covered with rare trees, palm-like cycads, tree ferns, podocarpus conifers and wild figs.

North of Lous Trichardt, the N1 passes by several striking **baobab trees**, all of which are protected as national monuments. A superb specimen can be spotted from the road, 5 km (3 miles) before the small town of Musina (formerly Messina).

Mapungubwe National Park

Overlooking the Limpopo River, some 75 km (46 miles) northwest of Musina, is Mapungubwe Hill, former site of an indigenous stone city that flourished from AD 950. Several artefacts unearthed at the site—most famously two gold statues of rhinoceros—indicate that this ancient city's wealth was built on gold, which was mined locally, transported by land to Indian Ocean ports such as Sofala and Kilwa, then shipped to Arabia. The stone city, whose contemporary name is unrecorded, was abandoned circa AD 1200, when its residents evidently relocated further north to build the more impressive stone city of Great Zimbabwe. Designated a UNESCO World Heritage Site in 2002, Mapungubwe is now the centrepiece of an eponymous national park, which is also notable for its stirring views over the Limpopo and the presence of wildlife such as elephants and klipspringer.

Tzaneen

The main roads to the northern section of Kruger National Park lead from Polokwane through the Tzaneen region. The most beautiful route involves a detour over the **Magoebaskloof Pass**, crossing forests and tea plantations on the way, an area known as the "land of the silver mist". It takes in the pretty village of **Haenertsburg**, smothered in springtime by azaleas and flowering cherry trees.

Other sights on the way to Tzaneen are the artificial lake of the **Ebenezer Dam** surrounded by pine forest and eucalyptus plantations, and waterfalls at **Debengeni**, 80 m (262 ft) high.

Tzaneen is a charming place for an overnight stop in the middle of tobacco and coffee plantations, orchards and nut groves.

The beautiful Marico sunbird *(Cinnyris mariquensis)* drinks nectar and feeds on butterflies, bees and other insects.

istockphoto.com/Van den Berg

Mpumalanga

The countryside of Mpumalanga, "the place where the sun rises", formerly Eastern Transvaal, is well worth a visit in its own right; it lies conveniently on the main route from Pretoria or Johannesburg to the Kruger Park's southern section.

Blyde River Canyon

The Blyde River Nature Reserve is a botanical paradise, with rare plant species such as aloes, cycads, orchids and ferns to be seen as well as an abundance of wildlife including plentiful monkeys and several vociferous bird species. The Blyde River Canyon, with sheer cliffs of red and yellow sandstone rising to 800 m (2,600 ft) in places, cuts through the reserve for 26 km (16 miles). A number of walking trails offer tours of any length up to several days, with overnight huts provided. Signs of human occupation dating from the Stone Age have been found in the **Echo Caves**, on private property a 20-minute drive west of the reserve.

Huts and Potholes

The most stunning viewpoint over the Blyde River, situated alongside a trunk road, is the **Three Rondavels**, where three enormous rocks in the shape of African huts rise up from the cliffs some 700 m (2,300 ft) on the opposite side of the canyon. At the confluence of this waterway with the Treur River, **Bourke's Luck Potholes**, scoured out by the staggering force of the water during the summer rains, impress with their perfect circular shape. And from **God's Window**, you can look between the rocks as if from a casement in the sky to view the savannah of the lowveld, which sweeps eastward towards the Kruger National Park. Not far away, the granite column of **Pinnacle Rock** rises like an exclamation mark above the delights of this favourite region of walkers and horsemen.

A Water World

The waters themselves play no small part in nature's spectacle. The magnificent 80-m (263-ft) **Berlin Falls** plunging from the mountain into a deep pool and the nearby horseshoe **Lisbon Falls** both afford extensive views over the wild, rocky landscapes of the canyon. The most-visited falls of the area are the twin cascades which pour into the **Mac Mac Pools**. The curious name is said to come from the large number of Scots who came to seek their fortune during the gold rush. The pure waters of these forest pools offer a blissful swim after a hot drive. Unlike most rivers in the region, they are free from the bilharzia parasite.

Pilgrim's Rest

The small town of Pilgrim's Rest was built in 1873 by the first gold rush pioneers. For practical purposes the gold finally ran out a century later, but what might easily have become a ghost town was carefully preserved. The historic atmosphere is maintained in an old mine, restored 19th-century tin houses and rudimentary shops. Some of the miners' cottages have been converted into hotel rooms, while demonstrations of gold-panning help to recreate the good old days.

To the east, Sabie is a pretty forestry town situated at the base of the region's tallest peak, Mount Anderson.

Mbombela

Formerly known as Nelspruit, Mbombela is the modern capital of Mpumalanga, a rapidly expanding city that services an area known for its production of nuts and citrus fruits, lying between the Kruger National Park and Swaziland. It was one of the venues for the 2010 FIFA World Cup, and a new stadium was built.

The **Lowveld National Botanical Garden**, set on the banks of the Crocodile River on the northern outskirts of town, is planted with an interesting selection of tropical trees—including baobabs and cycads—and is also host to a wide variety of colourful birds.

The road west back to Pretoria passes through the territory of the Southern Ndebele peoples. At the **Botshabelo Nature Reserve**, 15 km (9 miles) from Middelburg, a village and museum are dedicated to the Ndebele's appealing crafts, while a small game sanctuary protects, among other things, a herd of the endemic black wildebeest.

Kruger National Park

The Kruger National Park is South Africa's premier game viewing destination, home to 138 mammal species including aardvark, buffalo, cheetah, elephant, giraffe, hippopotamus, hyena, impala, leopard, lion, rhinoceros—and so on through the alphabet all the way to zebra. More than 100 different types of reptile are present, too. Extending over 19,000 sq km (7,335 sq miles), the park has recently become the cornerstone of the much larger **Great Limpopo Trans-Frontier Park**, which also incorporates Limpopo National Park in Mozambique and Gonarezhou National Park in Zimbabwe.

Divided between the provinces of Limpopo and Mpumalanga, the park contains around a dozen large rest camps, most of which offer comfortable and affordable bungalows with all modern conveniences, as well as campsites, shops and restaurants. Unlike many other African parks, the Kruger is also very easy to get around in a rented or private vehicle, with in excess of 2,500 km (1,560 miles) of well-maintained asphalt and dirt roads to explore.

For those who prefer a guided safari and luxury accommodation, several private concessions now operate in the Kruger, running along similar lines to the private reserves outside the park, but generally more affordably priced. These include Singita Lebombo, Rhino Walking Safaris and Lukimbi in the south/central region, and Pafuri and the Outpost in the north.

Southern Region
The park is conventionally divided into three zones, each with a distinct ecology and character. The southern section is the most popular with locals and tourists, not least because of its relative proximity to Gauteng and wide choice of accommodation. Rest camps include **Skukuza** (the largest and best-equipped in the park), **Lower Sabie** (unmatched location for game drives), **Crocodile Bridge** (small, intimate, and in an area

istockphoto.com/Gallas

istockphoto.com/Garry

Bourke's Luck Potholes in the Blyde River Canyon, named after a gold digger who staked a claim nearby. | The elephant has right of way in Kruger National Park.

istockphoto.com/Garry

known for rhino sightings), **Pretoriuskop** and **Bergendal**.

Characterized by dense acacia scrub and bisected by the Sabi River, the southern sector probably offers the best general game viewing in the park, with lion, wild dog, elephant and rhinoceros often seen alongside large herds of greater kudu and impala.

Central Region
More open in character, the central region is still reasonably accessible from Gauteng, and has some of the nicest rest camps in the park. **Satara**, though rather large and impersonal, lies in excellent lion and cheetah country, often frequented by large herds of zebra and wildebeest. **Olifants**, perched on a cliff above a river of the same name, is arguably the most spectacular camp of the lot. On the banks of the Letaba River, the **Letaba camp** is the favourite of many regulars, for its intimate feel, lovely setting and abundant game.

Northern Region
Favoured by the cognoscenti is the somewhat remote northern

istockphoto.com/Richter

The flower of the poisonous impala lily *(Adenium multiflorum)*. | Oxpeckers have a delightful diet of ticks, earwax and dandruff, feeding exclusively on the backs of large mammals.

sector, which is characterized by thick mopane woodland, and serviced by only a few small rest camps, of which Shingwedzi and Punda Maria both stand out. Although the northern circuit harbours lesser densities of game, its wilderness character more than compensates, and the concentrations of animals and birds along the Pafuri and Shingwedzi Rivers can be astounding.

Birdlife

The Kruger is mainly visited for its large mammals, but it's also a prime birding spot, with over 500 species recorded, of which the lovely lilac-breasted roller and white-fronted bee-eater routinely delight visitors. The park is a stronghold for several large birds —martial eagle, southern ground hornbill, secretary bird and kori bustard, for instance—that are increasingly rare outside protected areas.

Sabi Sands Game Reserve

Sabi Sands is a jointly administered block of private reserves that shares its unfenced eastern border with the southern Kruger Park, and protects a broadly similar range of large mammals and birds.

Several small luxury lodges lie within the reserve—the world-renowned **Sabi Sabi**, **Singida** and **Londolozi** among them—offering the alluring combination of five-star bush accommodation, superb food and wine, and probably the best Big Five game-viewing in Africa. Most of the lodges offer a similar package, with two daily game drives in an open safari vehicle, accompanied by a knowledgeable ranger and experienced tracker, following the rough roads that characterize the reserve and occasionally crashing through the bush in pursuit of a special sighting.

The reserve is famed for its superb big cat sightings: it's not unusual to see lion, cheetah and leopard in the course of one game drive, and the latter are incredibly habituated. Rhino, wild dog and elephant are also regularly encountered. The more intrepid can go on a bush walk with an expert guide, not only a good opportunity to concentrate on plants, birds and insects, but also offering a chance of a heart-stopping close encounter with a lion or buffalo.

MalaMala Game Reserve

Sandwiched between the Kruger Park and Sabi Sands, this is the largest private reserve in the region, covering 13,300 ha and with more than 20 km (12 miles) of Sabi River frontage. It is justifiably renowned, and there is simply no finer place in Africa for leopard sightings.

Durban's rickshaw drivers dress to match their vehicles.

Huber/PictureFinders

KwaZulu-Natal

KwaZulu-Natal assumed its present shape in 1994 following the amalgamation of the apartheid-era province of Natal and the nominally self-governing former "homeland" of KwaZulu (literally Place of the Zulu). The western boundary of KwaZulu-Natal is formed by the majestic uKhahlamba-Drakensberg Mountains, while the east coast is washed by the waters of the Indian Ocean.

Vasco da Gama sailed past present-day Durban on Christmas Day of 1497 and named the port Natalia, but it was only in the 1820s that the first European traders, hunters and ivory merchants settled in the area. Port Natal and its nascent harbour town were subsequently renamed Durban in honour of Sir Benjamin d'Urban, the governor of the Cape responsible for the British annexation of the area, but Da Gama's original name has been kept for the province. Many of the early engagements of the Anglo-Boer War were fought in the western part of Natal: Colenso, Spioenkop and the siege of Ladysmith.

Durban

Occupied by the Boers during the Great Trek, then retaken by the British, Durban is the nation's largest port. It now falls within the eThekweni metropolitan municipality, but the city itself is still known as Durban. This is the biggest city in KwaZulu-Natal and the third-largest in South Africa, with some 2 million inhabitants. Impregnated with the scent of spices, Durban is also a sort of Indian Ocean version of Miami. You might easily get the impression that the entire population is devoted to sun-and-sea worship. Surfers brave the breakers along its endless string of dazzling beaches, while golfers confront the perfectly tended fairways.

The Sea Front

Durban's sea front is vaguely reminiscent of the Bay of Nice, or Copacabana. Its Golden Mile stretches for not just one but five miles (8 km), a parade of international restaurants, hotels and well-guarded beaches. An amusement park with miniature trains, boat-trips and merry-go-rounds enlivens this world of concrete high-rises and swimming pools, made colourful by the stalls of Zulu women selling handicrafts. Rickshaw drivers in Zulu dress ply up and down the beach front.

The port area is undergoing attractive redevelopment. Harbour cruises are a highlight.

uShaka Marine World

Families visiting sunny Durban enjoy watching the troupes of dolphins, killer whales, seals and penguins going through their paces. A bewildering variety of marine life is on display here, including tropical fish, sharks and turtles.

MiniTown
Further north on Snell Parade, this attraction displays replicas of Durban's important buildings on a 1:24 scale. Children love the tiny fun fair and circus, and there is a working harbour, moving planes and a railway.

Market, mosque and temple
As the most easterly of South Africa's large cities, Durban is fittingly the place to find Indian markets. **Victoria Street Market**, set up in a domed building that looks like a Maharajah's palace, is an absolute must. Its stalls and shops offer all the spices of the Orient — and quite a few of its manufactured goods, too.

The oriental influence is further illustrated by sanctuaries such as the vast golden-domed **Juma Masjid** on Dr Jusuf Dadoo Street, rebuilt several times since it was founded in the early 1880s, resulting in a mixture of styles. The **Indian Temple of Understanding**, further south at Chatsworth, near the road to the airport, was built by the Krishna Consciousness Movement. This Hindu temple is a masterpiece of religious architecture, with an opulent interior. The Indian population first came to South Africa in the 1860s to work in the sugar-cane plantations. The population now numbers over a million and is influential in local commerce. Mahatma Gandhi began his political career here as a lawyer campaigning for the rights of Indian people.

Town Centre
The impressive **City Hall** marks the centre of Durban and houses the Public Library, the Durban Art Gallery and the Natural Science Museum, which has a good collection of ornithological exhibits, including a stuffed dodo. The **Playhouse** theatre complex in two former cinemas at 231 Smith St is the centre of the province's dramatic art.

The business area behind the seafront is livelier by night than by day, with its many bars and clubs. A stroll through the town can be rounded off by boarding a boat at **Victoria Embankment** for a trip round the harbour. From the water you can take a look at the **Da Gama Clock**, a gift to the city of Durban from the people of Portugal in 1897 to commemorate the 400th anniversary of Vasco da Gama's arrival on these shores.

Zululand
Northern KwaZulu-Natal, generally referred to as Zululand, is

one of the most exciting parts of South Africa to explore in a private vehicle, boasting fine game reserves, as well as a succession of lush sub-tropical beaches — and, of course, lying at the historical heart of the great Zulu Kingdom.

Hluhluwe-Imfolozi Game Reserve

The largest and oldest of the Zululand game reserves, Hluhluwe and Imfolozi (both named after the rivers that run through them) were proclaimed separately in 1897 but are now linked by a corridor of state-owned land and managed as a single unit.

The 96,000-ha complex is best known for its critical role in rhinoceros conservation. White rhino would today almost certainly be extinct were it not for Imfolozi — when the reserve was proclaimed, only 30 survived in the wild in South Africa — while Hluhluwe has long been a major stronghold for black rhino. Not only does this reserve protect the world's highest densities of wild rhinoceros, but almost 5,000 of its rhino (including the founders of the present-day Kruger Park population) have been relocated to other game reserves over the years.

Hluhluwe in particular is one of the most scenic of South African reserves, an undulating landscape of rolling hills covered

Zulu dancing. Zulu games and dances are intertwined, children being introduced very early in life to their traditional tribal choreography. Every gesture is imbued with significance and translates an idea. Dances are the means of making a covenant with the gods, of consecrating the initiation of boys and of girls into adulthood, of recounting an adventure, of celebrating an exploit. The rhythms bring happiness and symbolize hope.

While dancing, the Zulu child plays at being a soldier, bringing to life again the rites of the glorious warriors of old. Small boys, each holding his shield and a stick, sometimes even an assegai, take their weight on one leg and swing the other high to the sky before crashing it back down to the ground, as if trying to crack the very earth wide open.

Huber/PictureFinders

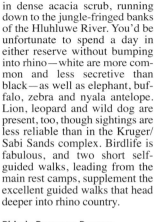

in dense acacia scrub, running down to the jungle-fringed banks of the Hluhluwe River. You'd be unfortunate to spend a day in either reserve without bumping into rhino — white are more common and less secretive than black — as well as elephant, buffalo, zebra and nyala antelope. Lion, leopard and wild dog are present, too, though sightings are less reliable than in the Kruger/Sabi Sands complex. Birdlife is fabulous, and two short self-guided walks, leading from the main rest camps, supplement the excellent guided walks that head deeper into rhino country.

Phinda Resource Reserve

Phinda was established in 1991 when &Beyond (formerly CC Africa, founder of the legendary Londolozi Private Reserve in Sabi Sands) acquired some 14,000 ha of degraded farmland and hunting concessions abutting the Greater St Lucia Wetland (now iSimangaliso). Over the next couple of years, elephant, lion, rhino, cheetah and buffalo were re-introduced to the fenced reserve, which already protected small populations of leopard and

A cheetah cub in his grassland playground. | **A hippo opens wide to show his displeasure, in Hluhluwe-Imfolozi Game Reserve.**

various antelope, and four small, exclusive lodges were constructed. One of the most carefully managed reserves in Africa, Phinda is too compact and contained to be regarded as true wilderness, but the expertly guided game drives—in open vehicles—are reliably superlative. The odds of seeing the Big Five over a couple of days are very good, and close encounters with cheetah are something of a speciality.

Ndumo Game Reserve

Nudged against the Mozambique border, this small reserve is primarily known for its diverse avifauna. Regarded by many as the country's finest birdwatching site, Ndumo's dense scrub and fig forests harbour numerous species with a limited range in South Africa, and the network of rivers, swamps and lakes teem with water associated birds. Boat trips along this labyrinth of waterways reliably offer dentist-eye views of hippos and crocs, while game drives and guided walks often result in close-up encounters with giraffe, black rhino and nyala antelope.

Tembe Elephant Reserve

Situated a short distance east of Ndumo, Tembe was proclaimed and fenced off in 1983 to protect a herd of about 150 elephant that formerly ranged between South Africa and Mozambique. Serviced by a small tented camp, this reserve harbours several other large mammals, as well as many bird species more normally associated with Ndumo—there's talk of linking the two reserves eventually. Access is by 4x4 only.

uMkhuze Game Reserve

Another compact but thrilling game reserve, uMkhuze is a reliable place to see rhino, giraffe and the lovely nyala antelope. A series of hides overlooking the waterholes is particularly rewarding for photography in the early dry season, when the water attracts a steady stream of game. A beautiful lake in the south of the reserve, encircled by tall stands of yellow fever trees and low hills, is scenically reminiscent of East Africa's Rift Valley, and often harbours large numbers of hippo and pelican. The nearby fig forest is a treat for birders, as is the self-guided walk around the main rest camp.

iSimangaliso Wetland Park

The entire coastline running north of Cape Vidal to the Mozambican border is now part of the iSimangaliso Wetland Park (formerly the Greater St Lucia Wetland Park, proclaimed a UNESCO World Heritage Site in 1999). Here, Africa's most southerly coral reefs support a wide range of colourful tropical fish, and **Sodwana Bay** in particular is very popular with South African divers, snorkellers and anglers. The expansive, pristine sandy beaches that characterize this stretch of Indian Ocean coastline also form an important breeding side for endangered marine turtles, while the coastal scrub hosts several localized birds and troops of monkey. **Lake Sibaya**, a short distance inland, is — incredibly — the largest natural freshwater body in South Africa, with 200 or more resident hippopotamus. Tourist development in the area, not resort-like in any conventional sense, is epitomized by the game lodge-like feel of the superb, exclusive Rocktail Bay Lodge, close to the Mozambique border.

The village of **St Lucia** is the obvious base for exploring the area, being located at the mouth of the estuary. This is South Africa's largest estuarine system, dominated by a lagoon 50 km (30 miles) long that is fed by half a dozen rivers and divided from the Indian Ocean by a terrestrial sliver of tall dunes swathed in lush coastal forest. In addition to having a fine beach, albeit more popular with anglers than sunbathers, St Lucia is equipped with plenty of accommodation. It also forms the starting point for launch trips on the estuary (prodigious hippos, crocs and waterbirds) and for

self-guided walks among the zebra and wildebeest that frequent a small bordering game reserve.

A superb scenic drive on an indifferent road between the estuary and the ocean leads north from Saint Lucia to the idyllic beach and rest camp at **Cape Vidal**, passing through grassy swamps frequented by large herds of reedbuck and a series of bird hides overlooking estuary.

On the western shore of the estuary, **Charters Creek** rest camp stands in a patch of thick coastal scrub inhabited by warthog, the diminutive red duiker and a variety of forest birds — listen out for the cat-in-a-mangle wailing of the preposterous trumpeter hornbill. For keen walkers, the nearby **False Bay Reserve** has two excellent day trails through a tract of dunes and coastal bush teeming with large mammals and birds.

Ulundi

The former administrative capital of the defunct KwaZulu "homeland", Ulundi (literally High Place) lies inland of the Hluhluwe-Imfolozi Game Reserve about 200 km (125 miles) northeast of Durban. Of greater interest than Ulundi itself is the **Ondoni Heritage Park & KwaZulu Cultural Museum**, built on the site of King Cetshwayo's former royal enclosure a mere 5 km (3 miles) from town. Razed by British troops in

1879, Cetshwayo's enclosure has been partially restored, while the main museum houses an absorbing miscellany of Zulu artefacts and historical displays—and inexpensive on-site accommodation in traditional Zulu beehive huts.

Shakaland and other cultural villages

Several traditional Zulu villages (*kraal* in Afrikaans) may be visited in KwaZulu-Natal Province. Shakaland is the most firmly established of these, 15 km (9 miles) from Eshowe and about 150 km (94 miles) north of Durban. King Shaka (1788–1828) has been called "Africa's Napoleon". His *kraal* was completely recreated for the film *Shaka Zulu* and is now run by a hotel chain—you can book accommodation. The traditions and costumes of the Zulu people are presented in a happy atmosphere. You can sample local food and watch the many demonstrations of Zulu dances and rites. Despite historical inaccuracies, the village is attractive and provides employment for many local people.

Shakaland can become very overcrowded with day trippers in the high season, but two other conceptually similar hotels in the Eshowe region offer an equally insightful and somewhat lower key cultural experience. **Kwabhe-**

istockphoto.com/Parnell

In the kraals you will see traditional huts made of straw.

kithunga is a small, private lodge where visitors can spend time with a traditional Zulu family that's lived in the area for as long as anybody can remember. More memorable still is **Simunye**, spectacularly set on a cliff overlooking a traditional Zulu *kraal*—visitors are transferred to the lodge in a traditional ox-cart, and the more adventurous can opt to sleep in a hut within the *kraal* rather than in the more conventional tourist rooms.

Military history buffs will want to visit the Zulu War battlefields, including **Isandlwana** and **Rorke's Drift**. Close together, east of Dundee, they were the scenes of many acts of courage as well as disastrous losses on both sides. You'll find guided tours and maps at the tourist offices.

Eshowe

The small town of Eshowe was the first administrative centre of

British Zululand. The British fort of Nongqayi, built in 1883, has been refurbished as the **Nongqayi Village Historical Museum**. Also of interest is the **Vukani Cultural Museum**, which houses a superb collection of traditional handcrafts and artefacts.

The lush, shady **Dhlinza Forest Reserve**, in the heart of this pretty town, is the site of the country's canopy walk, which winds upwards for 125 m towards a platform 20 m (65 ft) high that offers great views into the tree tops. Dhlinza is a good place to see the tiny blue duiker and a wide selection of forest birds.

Closer to the coast, the **Umlalazi Nature Reserve**, bordering the small resort town of Mtunzini, might be rather low-key by comparison to the game reserves of northern Zululand, but it still has much to offer keen walkers. Particularly rewarding is a foot trail through the mangroves, where one is likely to encounter hermit crabs, mudskippers (a fish that can live on land) and the localized mangrove kingfisher—most likely to be detected by its shrill call. A stand of raffia palms within the reserve is the only breeding site in the country for the majestic palm-nut vulture.

Pietermaritzburg

Although most tours of Zululand return to Durban along the N2 highway in a matter of hours, it's also possible to take the road through the interior, allowing two days for the complete circuit including the visit to Shakaland. Driving through the hilly country of Zululand, you will come across other communities and kraals such as the **Assegai** and **PheZulu** safari parks by taking the route through the Valley of a Thousand Hills between Pietermaritzburg and the coast.

Smaller and far sleepier than Durban, Pietermaritzburg is nevertheless the provincial capital of KwaZulu-Natal. Nestled in a lush, misty valley in the southern part of the province, the town has a compact centre that has retained many old buildings, allowing you to feel something of the atmosphere of the era of the Voortrekkers who arrived at this fertile site in 1837. The settlement they founded, with wide streets and pretty gardens, was named in honour of two of their leaders, Piet Retief and Gerrit Maritz.

Around Town

The **Voortrekker House**, the oldest two-storey dwelling in town, has been carefully restored and authentically furnished.

In 1842 the British annexed the young Natal Republic, set up a military garrison and chose Pietermaritzburg as the administrative centre of the new colony of Natal. A good number of buildings dating from the colonial era have survived, including the mosques and Hindu temples of the Indian traders, as well as the **Macrorie House Museum** containing furniture and clothing from the Victorian age.

The city is also home to the **Natal Museum**, whose extensive natural history and ethnographic collections rank among the finest in the country, and the **Voortrekker/Msunduzi Museum**, which celebrates the province's colourful history and cultural variety.

The **Town Hall**, a Victorian building where 12 bells ring out from the top of its 47-m (155-ft) tower, is said to be the largest all-brick building in the southern hemisphere. Edwardian and Victorian façades rise above narrow lanes paved in the same red brick, and even the schools have made it a point of honour to maintain the great British traditions.

A broad panorama of the town can be seen from the belvedere and landmark table at **World's View** on the Howick road, at an altitude of 305 m (1,000 ft).

Walks and Drives
The lush countryside surrounding Pietermaritzburg caters to every interest. The **Green Belt Trail** can be followed on foot or on horseback through areas of abundant plant and animal life. The **Midlands Meander** is a pleasant circuit through the Midlands towns and villages where there are many delightful restaurants, art galleries, and craft centres featuring weaving and pottery-making, notably around the town of **Nottingham Road**.

More than 200 species of bird have been recorded in the **Umgeni Valley**, while the magnificent **Howick Falls**, overlooked by the small town of the same name, plunge from a height of 100 m (328 ft) in an unspoilt setting with plentiful wildlife.

South Coast
Between Durban and Port Edward you have at least a hundred resorts to choose from. Well worth considering are **Amanzimtoti** and the **Nyoni Rocks** with 7 km (4 miles) of safe beaches; **Margate**, which gets the vote of the young crowd for its lively nightlife; and **Shelly Beach** for its abundance of seashells.

Vernon Crookes Nature Reserve
If you need a break from the sea, visit this haven for many birds— 300 species—together with animals such as eland, blue wildebeest, impala and zebra. With an area of 2,189 ha, the park is made up of open grassland and rolling hills, combined with coastal forest. In spring, the wild flowers are a delight to behold.

istockphoto.com/Focus_On_Nature

The Hole in the Wall has been gouged out by the waves.

Oribi Gorge
Near **Port Shepstone**, the ravine, 24 km (15 miles) long, shelters antelope, leopard and baboons between its majestic sandstone cliffs studded with clumps of euphorbia; eagles soar above.

Wild Coast
You can continue south beyond Port Edward along the spectacular Wild Coast as far as East London, crossing the old frontier of the former Transkei "homeland" on the way. Along some stretches the violence of the confrontation

of ocean and mountain is simply breathtaking. The pounding of wave against rock has created a giant hollow in the cliff face at **Hole in the Wall** near Mncwasa Point and Coffee Bay.

The most beautiful parts of this coastline have been made into nature reserves, but access is not always easy, as the topography has prevented construction of a road that clings to the shore.

uKhahlamba-Drakensberg Park
Running along the Lesotho frontier, the escarpment known to the Zulu as uKhahlamba (Barrier of Spears) and to Afrikaners as the Drakensberg (Dragon's Mountain) rises to 3,482 m (11,424 ft), the highest point in Africa south of Kilimanjaro. The vertiginous walls of basalt and rolling foothills have been amalgamated into Africa's largest protected montane wilderness, one of only 27 UNESCO World Heritage sites listed for both natural and cultural significance.

Royal Natal National Park
This northern sector of uKhahlamba-Drakensberg, proclaimed in 1916, contains some of Africa's most spectacular scenery. Its principal feature is the natural amphitheatre, a basalt arc 8 km (5 miles) long, guarded by towering peaks, the Sentinel, 3,165 m (10,400 ft) and the Eastern But-

tress, 3,047 m (9,997 ft). A number of domes rise from its summit. The largest dome, Mont-aux-Sources (literally, Spring Mountain), 3,284 m (10,770 ft), is the source of the River Tugela which falls more than 2,000 m (6,560 ft) in a spectacular series of cascades down to the plateau below.

You don't have to be a mountain-climber to enjoy the park; there are easy walking trails, as well as more challenging routes. While you walk the trails you are likely to encounter Zulu women cutting reeds for basket-weaving.

This way, that way? Read the signs in the Drakensberg mountains.

Giant's Castle Game Reserve

In central uKhahlamba-Drakensberg, the Giant's Castle reserve supports a range of antelope—notably eland. A major attraction for ornithologists is a so-called "vulture restaurant" where carrion is left out to attract scavenging birds. The endemic Cape vulture and rare bearded vulture (or lammergeyer) are both regular visitors to the site.

However, the reserve is chiefly known for its many caves decorated with San rock paintings. Richly supplied with game and with plentiful water, the uKhahlamba-Drakensberg mountains were once a safe haven for the peaceful San who inhabited southern Africa for thousands of years before the arrival of the first Europeans. Chased from their hunting grounds, initially by more warlike pastoral tribes and later by European settlers, these hardy hunter-gatherers left behind a rich collection of rock art illustrating the essentials of their daily life. In rust-red, purple-brown and ochre, their murals most frequently depict men and animals (usually eland), warriors engaged in battle, or shaman performing mystical trance rituals. According to the experts, the most ancient of these works of art were created 27,000 years ago. More recent paintings depicting ox-carts, men with rifles on horseback and the like demonstrate that the artists were still active at the time of the Great Trek.

One of the most fascinating panels contains 546 paintings and is only 2 km (just over a mile) from a camp where you can stay overnight in a thatched hut. In another cave, as many as 750 rock paintings have been counted.

The Basotho women decorate their huts inside and out, in a style that still persists throughout the Free State.

Free State

The Free State, founded more than a century ago, was originally named the Orange Free State after the Orange River on its southern boundary. It is a vast region, occupying the highveld of the central plateau to the south of Johannesburg, and sharing its frontier with Gauteng, Mpumalanga, KwaZulu-Natal, Eastern and Northern Cape and North West provinces as well as the independent Lesotho enclave. The granary of the nation, the Free State is characterized by immense plains of wheat and maize, and it is also rich in natural resources such as gold, diamonds, uranium and—more humbly—coal.

Bloemfontein

The prosperous city of Bloemfontein, capital of this attractive province, was founded by trekboeren in the 1840s as capital of the Orange Free State. It served as a centre of British operations during the Anglo-Boer War. The name literally means "spring of flowers", though it could well have been named after one Jan Bloem, who lived here before the Voortrekkers. The column and mosaic of the Fontein (fountain) mark the spring which was the origin of the town.

The city now forms part of the municipality of Mangaung, a Sesotho name that means Place of Cheetahs. No big cats live wild in the vicinity today, but rehabilitated orphans can be seen at the **Cheetah Experience**, 5 km (3 miles) from the city centre. The more central **Franklin Game Reserve** on Naval Hill offer the opportunity to walk among giraffes, zebras and other ungulates.

The **First Raadsaal Museum**, a thatched adobe construction with beaten dung floor, dates from 1849 and is the oldest of a handful of 19th-century buildings close to the central square. The Legislative Assembly (Volksraad) used to meet here, but it became too small for the flourishing community and three more assembly rooms were built in succession.

Housed in a building dating to 1877, the **National Museum of Bloemfontein** is particularly strong on archaeology such as Karoo fossils, but it also houses an interesting selection of natural history displays and traditional cultural artefacts.

Bloemfontein is the judicial capital of South Africa. The **Appeal Court**, seat of the country's highest judicial authority, boasts several richly furnished rooms. The old **Presidency**, which was built in 1885 in the Victorian style now houses a collection of presidential documents tracing the history of the Boer Republic of Orange Free State.

Before the British occupation of the town in 1900, the Assembly met in the **Fourth Raadsaal**, a handsome red-brick building with Doric columns and a domed tower and still in use as a government building.

A 36.5-m (120-ft) obelisk, the **National Women's Memorial** honours the 26,000 women and children who died of disease in the concentration camps of the Anglo-Boer War (1899–1902).

Willem Pretorius Game Reserve

To the north, close to the Johannesburg road, the reserve, encircling the great lake formed by the Allemanskraal Dam, is particularly rich in white rhinoceros. They happily coexist with many other wildlife species. Because of the sparse vegetation it's relatively easy to see and photograph the animals, and a high hill dominating the savannah makes a perfect observation point.

White and black rhinoceros can readily be distinguished from each other by the respective shapes of their mouths. The white rhino has wide, square lips suited to cropping grass, while the slightly smaller (and significantly more pugnacious) black rhino has a narrow mouth, overhung by a hooked upper lip, reflecting its browsing habits.

Ladybrand

The **Catharina Brand Museum** displays a collection of fossils, painted rocks, Bushman tools and musical instruments which date from the Stone Age. They may inspire you to visit some of the archaeological sites of the region, among which **Rose Cottage Cave** and **Modderpoort Cave Church** are the most significant. Countless scenic beauty spots stretch along the nearby frontier with Lesotho as far as Harrismith.

Golden Gate National Park

Named after a spectacular rock formation, Golden Gate is located at an altitude of over 2,000 m (6,600 ft) on the northwest slopes of the uKhahlamba-Drakensberg. In a prodigious mountain setting, Cape vultures, black eagles, bearded vultures (or lammergeyers) and numerous other species make it a thrilling venue for birdwatchers. Reached from the small towns of Clarens or Harrismith, the **Basotho Cultural Village** showcases the lifestyle and architecture of the South Sotho, from the 16th century to the present. On the Matlakeng Herbal Trail you will learn how various roots, leaves, grasses and bark are used to cure all kinds of ailments.

Brandwater Hiking Trail

Fouriesburg marks the start of the trail that leads to the Salpeterkrans limestone cave, the largest in the southern hemisphere. The region caters chiefly to hikers.

LESOTHO

Landlocked—in fact, surrounded on all sides by South African soil—Lesotho is a small, mountainous and predominantly rural country, most of which stands at an elevation of above 2,000 m. The population, estimated at 2.5 million, is comprised almost entirely of the Basotho, whose ancestors probably migrated to the highlands in the 16th century, and were consolidated into a unified nation under King Moshoeshoe in the 1820s, largely in response to the threat posed by their militant Zulu neighbours.

Never colonized as such—possibly because the land was too poor to appeal to settlers—Lesotho became a British protectorate in the late 19th century. Since independence in 1966, Lesotho has been economically dependent on its larger, wealthier neighbour, surviving on subsistence agriculture, international aid, and money sent home by migrant workers, many of them in South Africa's gold mines. Lesotho, like Swaziland, remains one of Africa's few tribally homogenous kingdoms, although it differs from Swaziland in that an elected government exists to reign in the power of the monarchy.

Inspirational montane scenery and limited development outside of major towns, together with the legendary friendliness of the blanket-clad rural Basotho, combine to make Lesotho a highly rewarding hiking and

Looking down the road to the Sani Pass.

istockphoto.com/Badenhorst

trekking destination, particularly for those seeking unforced contact with traditional cultures. For all that, few overseas tourists cross into the kingdom, if only for the simple reason that it is rather inaccessible from any established South African tourist circuit (the only surfaced roads into Lesotho approach the western border from the seldom-visited eastern Free State). Outside the capital, few hotels meet accepted international standards. Lesotho, in essence, is a destination less suited to conventional tourism than it is to intrepid independent travellers, hikers and other outdoor enthusiasts.

Maseru and surroundings

Set at an elevation of 1,650 m (4,513 ft), only 20 km (12 miles) by road from Ladybrand in the Free State, Maseru made headlines in 1998 when South African troops controversially crossed the border to put down a revolt sparked by a contested election that had taken place earlier that year. Maseru was never the most prepossessing of capital cities, and the still visible scars of the destructive looting that followed the South African invasion have scarcely improved matters. Most travellers pass through the city as quickly as possible, but it does boast a decent tourist information office, as well as a scattering of international quality hotels. A more appealing place to stay is the elevated plateau of Thaba Bosiu (Mountain of Night), which is situated only 15 km (9 miles) from the modern capital. A national monument held sacred by Basotho traditionalists, this mountain was the military stronghold from where King Moshoeshoe forged the Basotho Kingdom in the 19th century, and where he was buried after his death in 1870.

A Sotho elder in a typical conical straw hat (woven by the men).

Pony treks

The most attractive way to explore the steep contours of rural Lesotho is to travel as the locals do: wrapped in a blanket on the back of a sturdy Basotho pony. One convenient base for treks is the Basotho Pony Trekking Centre, situated alongside the road to Roma, a university town 35 km (22 miles) east of Maseru. Also very popular is Malealea Lodge, which lies in a part of the southern highlands studded with mysterious rock art sites, tumbling waterfalls and rare plants such as the endemic spiral aloe. Both organizations arrange a variety of half-day treks to close-by waterfalls, as well as longer trips (up to a week in duration) generally terminating at Semonkong—site of the spectacular 190-m (623-ft) Lebihan Falls, the tallest waterfall in South Africa.

Sehlabathebe National Park

Lesotho's only national park, Sehlabathebe runs along the eastern border with the KwaZulu-Natal's uKhahlamba-Drakensberg Park. A wild, remote landscape of timeworn sandstone formations and caves, it is towered over by a trio of jagged peaks known as the Three Bushmen. The main attractions of this remote park are the scenery (sweeping views to the escarpment base) and the wonderful off-the-beaten-track hiking possibilities. Some large mammals remain, too, most notably eland and grey rhebok, even the stray leopard. Birdlife includes the exquisite malachite sunbird, the mighty lammergeyer and the localized bald ibis.

The spiral aloe can turn clockwise or anticlockwise.

The Apple Express puffs over a bridge of stunning design.

Eastern Cape

Halfway between Durban and the Cape of Good Hope, the Eastern Cape, both maritime and mountainous, provides a transition between the tropical exuberance of KwaZulu-Natal and the delights of the Western Cape.

East London

Despite its name, the relic of its origin as a British military supply post set up in 1848, East London has a strong link to the region's German settlers who arrived ten years later. They have their own memorial monument here and, in homage to their home country, founded the nearby towns of Potsdam, Berlin and Braunschweig.

The bustling activity on East London's Buffalo River contrasts with the tranquillity of the lagoons and the long beaches of the biggest river port in South Africa.

Around Town

From East London's beginnings, some 19th- and early 20th-century buildings remain in the city centre around the junction of the main shopping thoroughfares of Oxford Street and Fleet Street. On the latter is the Lock Street Gaol, built in 1880 as a garrison fort and transformed into South Africa's first women's prison. Now it is a shopping centre with bars in some of the old cells.

At the north end of Oxford Street, the **East London Museum** features a famous coelacanth fish caught by a local fisherman in 1938. Thought to have survived 250 million years until it died out 40 million years ago, this fish, previously known to science only in fossil form, is on show here nicely stuffed, 1.6 m (5 ft) long, with all its teeth. The extinct dodo bird is also exhibited with the world's only known extant egg and a life-size model of the creature which was hunted to extinction in Mauritius by European sailors. The museum also has interesting sections devoted to traditional Xhosa lifestyle and the early British and German settlers.

Over the two-tiered bridge across the mouth of the Buffalo River, **Latimers Landing** has been redeveloped as a shopping and restaurant area with facilities for boat and yacht cruises around the harbour.

Along the seafront esplanade overlooking Shipwreck Bay, the **Aquarium** boasts over 100 species of tropical fish and other marine creatures. Seals and penguins perform daily.

Behind the aquarium is the **German Settlers' Memorial**, paying tribute to the 2,315 men, women and children who arrived here in 1857 as part of the Deutsche Legion to develop the trade potential of the port and hinterland.

Grahamstown

Best known as the site of Rhodes University and the National Arts Festival (held over 10 days every July), Grahamstown was founded by the 1820 Settlers. It boasts several churches and other buildings dating to the mid-19th century. The **1820 Settlers Museum** contains displays and photographs relating to this period, while the **Albany Museum** is strong on precolonial history and rock art.

Port Alfred

Another 1820 Settler town that is bypassed by most international tourists, Port Alfred has a lovely beachfront location straddling the shady banks of the Kowie River estuary south of Grahamstown. An excellent overnight canoe trail follows the Kowie River through lush riverine vegetation in the **Waters Meeting Nature Reserve**, while the **Alexandria Hiking Trail** at close-by Kenton-on-Sea is of interest for its tall dunes, coastal forest, and rich birdlife.

Port Elizabeth

The beaches and resorts of **Nelson Mandela Bay** (formerly Algoa Bay) are justifiably the pride and joy of the industrial city of Port Elizabeth. Some Victorian buildings, notably those in Donkin Street, contrast with an otherwise unattractive industrial centre. Sir Rufane Donkin, the founder of the town, named it Port Elizabeth after his wife. Its development began in about 1820, with the arrival of 4,000 British settlers. From the reptiles in **Snake Park** and the exotic birds in the **Tropical House** to the fishes and seals in the **Oceanarium**, there is plenty to keep you entertained in between outings to the beach.

Addo Elephant National Park

This park, 72 km (45 miles) north of Port Elizabeth, was gazetted in 1931 to protect the area's last few elephants. Its elephant population now stands at about 500, and the park has been expanded all the way to the coast. Lion, hyena and rhino have been reintroduced, while various antelope and 150 bird species occur naturally. A good road network emanates from the rest camp at the main entrance gate.

Close to Addo is the exclusive **Shamwari Game Reserve**; guided game drives in open vehicles usually sight lion, elephant, rhino and antelope.

Apple Express

If you're nostalgic for the days of steam, climb aboard the Apple Express. Established in 1903, this narrow-gauge line links Port Elizabeth with the town of **Loerie** via the superb countryside of the fruit-growing **Langkloof Valley**. Longer weekend trips are also run to **Assegaaibos Station** and the village of **Patensie**, a citrus farming community that is gateway to the **Baviaanskloof Mega Reserve**, one of the Cape Floral Region protected areas and on the UNESCO World Heritage list.

Graaff-Reinet

Some 270 km (170 miles) northwest of Port Elizabeth, Graaff-Reinet, founded in 1786, is the fourth-oldest European settlement in South Africa. The old town preserves 220 buildings and private dwellings, most of them listed as national monuments. They include Cape Dutch houses, Karoo flat-roofed cottages, Victorian villas, and a striking Dutch Reformed church modelled on Salisbury Cathedral. The town is in the centre of a region of widely scattered farmsteads. Merino sheep and angora goats graze the sparse vegetation; rainfall is uncertain and summer temperatures can reach 40°C (104°F).

Bordering Graaff-Reinet, the **Camdeboo National Park** (formerly Karoo Nature Reserve) embraces over 40,000 acres of rare plant-life, as well as zebra, antelope and wildebeest. Also within the park are the cathedral-like rock formations of the **Valley of Desolation**.

Mountain Zebra National Park

Near **Cradock**, a lively agricultural centre on the banks of the Great Fish River, the park was gazetted in 1937 to ensure the survival of the Cape mountain zebra, a race endemic to South Africa. Some 300 of these rare creatures roam the 280-sq-km (108-sq-mile) reserve, which is also home to red hartebeest, black wildebeest, springbok, and more than 200 species of birds. On the northern slopes of the Bankberg chain at an altitude of 2,000 m (6,600 ft), the park offers stunning panoramas of the Karoo.

The Xhosa. The Eastern Cape is the home of the Xhosa, second in number only to the Zulus among South Africa's tribal groups. They have spread far beyond this province, especially to the cities, and provided many of the political leaders who campaigned against apartheid, including Nelson Mandela. In rural areas, the Xhosa live in thatched, circular huts called rondavels and wear woollen scarves as turbans. The women often paint their faces with ochre and smoke long pipes; young unmarried men may be seen with their faces painted ghostly white. The Xhosa language with its characteristic clicking sounds and range of tones is easily recognized but hard to learn.

The strange Halfmens plant watches over the Richtersveld National Park.

Northern Cape

Bordered by Botswana and Namibia to the north, the Free State to the east and the Atlantic Ocean to the west, the Northern Cape is the largest province in South Africa, and the most sparsely settled, supporting a mere two percent of the national population. Arid, wild, in part desert, the region is off the tourist track, probably because of its distance from the big cities. Nevertheless, it is easily accessible and contains some of the most beautiful countryside in South Africa, several nature reserves, four major national parks, and a diamond town way over to the east on the Free State border.

Upington

This is the main travel lynchpin of the Northern Cape and the obvious springboard for visits to the region's national parks. Straddling the banks of the Orange River (the country's longest waterway), it's an attractive and welcoming town, though quite small, with the excellent **Kalahari-Oranje Museum** relating local history, in the former church and mission station on Schroder St.

Upington's legendary **Le Must Country Restaurant** ranks as one of the finest traditional Cape eateries in the entire country, while the **Oranjerivier Wine Cellars** cooperative produces an array of drinkable and reasonably priced wines.

The **Spitskop Nature Reserve** on the outskirts of Upington harbours herds of gemsbok and springbok.

In Keimos, 40 km (25 miles) further east, the **Tierberg Nature Reserve** consists of a steep hill swathed in spectral kokerbooms and colourful aloes, and affords memorable views over the Orange River and associated agricultural scheme.

Kuruman

Ideally situated to break up the long drive between Gauteng and Upington, Kuruman is arguably the most attractive town in the Northern Cape, centred on a tree-lined natural spring, **The Eye**, that yields more than 50,000 cubic litres of freshwater daily.

About 6 km (4 miles) north of town, the **Kuruman Mission** founded in 1821 by the Scots missionary Robert Moffat—with its stone buildings and shady orchards—has the aura of a misplaced English country church surrounded by arid semi-desert. The Kuruman Mission was Livingstone's first posting in Africa, and a plaque commemorates the tree under which he proposed to Moffat's daughter Mary, before they were wed in the mission church.

Two worthwhile attractions lie within easy day-tripping distance of Kuruman. The **Wonderwerk Cave**, on the Danielskuil Road, has

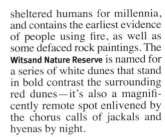

sheltered humans for millennia, and contains the earliest evidence of people using fire, as well as some defaced rock paintings. The **Witsand Nature Reserve** is named for a series of white dunes that stand in bold contrast the surrounding red dunes—it's also a magnificently remote spot enlivened by the chorus calls of jackals and hyenas by night.

Augrabies Falls National Park

About 120 km (75 miles) west of Upington, the waters of the Orange River plunge from a height of 56 m (184 ft) into a deep granite gorge to form the spectacular Augrabies Falls. The noise of the churning wall of water against the rock inspired the Khoikhoi to give the falls the name Augrabies, which in their tongue means "deafening". Look out for the colourful Augrabies and Cape flat lizards that scamper around the rocks above the waterfall.

Well-equipped with a camping area and bungalows, this national park is primarily of scenic interest, though it is populated by leopard, eland, rhinoceros, baboon, antelope and springbok.

Rock and rushing waters at Augrabies Falls, seen from a viewing platform, while a rainbow-like flat lizard (Platysaurus broadleyi) hunts for flies.

Hikers and strollers can take advantage of bountiful possibilities here, while night drives in an open vehicle offer a good chance of encountering a variety of nocturnal predators such as serval, caracal and genet. More adventurously, the **Augrabies Rush** is a half-day rafting trip that passes over a succession of grade 1 to 3 rapids upriver of the waterfall.

Kgalagadi Transfrontier Park

Slightly more than 200 km (120 miles) north of Upington by road, the former Kalahari Gemsbok National Park penetrates into the vast Kalahari Desert. The last refuge of the San, the desert also covers parts of Namibia and Botswana. The park, founded in 1931, was the second-largest in the country after the Kruger Park. In 2000, it was amalgamated with Botswana's Mabuasehube-Gemsbok National Park to form the co-managed Kgalagadi Transfrontier Park — at 38,000 sq km (14,800 sq miles) one of the largest protected wilderness areas in the world.

A mesmerizing landscape of tall red dunes, overhung by a seemingly permanent blue sky, and crossed by the Auob and Nossob Rivers (neither of which flow more often than once in ten years), this vast, arid park would be worth the admission price for its austere scenery alone. But it also happens to offer superb game viewing: lion, leopard, cheetah, spotted hyena, bat-eared fox and black-backed jackal are all like to be seen over the course of a few day's visit, while more elusive nocturnal predators include the aardwolf and brown hyena. The handsome gemsbok (oryx) for which the park was originally named is common, as are springbok, eland and wildebeest. The appealing ground

Take the "A" train. Several companies offer luxury on rails. The **Blue Train** travels in style between Cape Town and Pretoria, three times a week in each direction, and can be chartered for any other route in South Africa. **Rovos Rail** runs weekly trips between Pretoria and Cape Town via Kimberley and Matjiesfontein, as well as bi-monthly trips between Pretoria and Victoria Falls. There are also periodic trips from Pretoria to Durban, with two safaris en route, as well as trips in summer along the Garden Route from Cape Town to George. Special journeys are also organized, for instance from Cape Town to Dar es-Salaam in Tanzania. Historic steam locomotives are used wherever possible, and some of the carriages are 100 years old.

squirrel, meerkat and yellow mongoose thrive on the dunes, as does an excellent selection of dry-country birds and raptors.

Remote as it is, the Kgalagadi park is easily reached and explored in an ordinary saloon car, and three rest camps—**Twee Rivieren**, **Mata Mata** and **Nossob**—provide comfortable accommodation and a range of provisions. Also set within the park is the luxury **!Xaus Lodge**, which is owned by local San communities, as well as six small unfenced wilderness camps, each of which accommodates a maximum of eight guests.

Namaqualand

From the end of August until the end of September, after the southern hemisphere's springtime rains, the arid and inhospitable plains of Namaqualand—a region along the west coast, dividing the Western Cape from the Kalahari—are transformed into an immense carpet of some 4,000 species of vividly coloured flowers. The small country town of **Springbok** is a popular and well-equipped base from which to explore the area, as is the underrated **West Coast National Park** near Suldhana Bay, further south and more easily accessible from Cape Town.

At the northern tip of Namaqualand, up to the border with Namibia, is **Richtersveld National Park**. Half of the plant life found here, among its rocky mountains and immense sandy plains, is unique to this part of the world. The Halfmens *(Pachypodium namaquanum)*, a tree-like succulent with spiny trunks devoid of branches and crowned by a mop of leaves, is one of the most amazing plants on earth. Also called Elephant's Trunk, it grows to a height of 2 m (6.5 ft) and leans northwards to catch the sun in winter. The swollen trunk stores water, and in spring, tubular green flowers with crimson tips appear in the centre of the leaves.

Temperatures in summer can be extremely hot, but you can share the cool of the evening with the desert-loving springbok. Rise at dawn to drive along dry river beds and you may see a family of cheetah silhouetted against the skyline.

Kimberley

The capital of the Northern Cape, the legendary diamond town of Kimberley, on the border with Free State, is sure to interest anyone dazzled by sparklers. Four mines, made up of a labyrinth of galleries, own the lion's share of the glittering prizes.

The **Kimberley Big Hole** is the biggest man-made crater in the world. Since 1869 almost 28 million tons of "blue ground" have been shifted to obtain three tons of diamonds. The hole, now a waterlogged depression, covers an area of 27 acres. More than 30,000 miners worked here during the last century. The site and its surroundings, which you can reach on the Kimberley tram from City Hall, have been converted into an open-air museum where 50 or so cottages, shops, offices, pubs and churches have been scrupulously reconstructed as they would have appeared at the height of the diamond rush.

While you're here, visit the **San Cultural Project**, a living exhibition of the artefacts and way of life of an almost vanished people. Also worth an hour or two is the **Duggan-Cronin Gallery** on Egerton Road, which houses an illuminating collection of photographs of rural Africa taken all around the continent in the 1930s.

Further afield, **Driekopseiland**, 70 km (43 miles) from the town centre, is the site of over 3500 ancient rock engravings on exposed basement rock in the bed of the Riet River. Unlike other sites, the drawings here are 90 per cent geometric in design.

In spring the ground of Namaqualand is covered with a dense carpet of bright flowers. | The famed Big Hole in Kimberley. | Framed: a citrus-fruit seller keeps to the shade.

istockphoto.com/Roode

flickr.com/Irene2005

Huber/Ripani

Cheerful Bo-Kaap, an Islamic community on the slopes of Signal Hill.

Ariadne van Zandbergen

Western Cape

To many South Africans, the Western Cape is the most beautiful and most varied of all the South African provinces. This fertile countryside, washed on either side by the Indian and Atlantic oceans, like the Cape of Good Hope itself, was the place where the European history of South Africa began.

Cape Town

Surrounded by attractive and fashionable beaches, Cape Town is one of the most enticing cities in the world. It was founded in 1652 by Jan Van Riebeeck to provide a port where the ships of the Dutch East India Company could take on supplies on their voyage east. The setting, at the centre of exceptional sites of natural and cultural interest, couldn't be more spectacular. At the foot of the legendary Table Mountain, with ocean waves breaking on its shores, Cape Town's old colonial houses rub shoulders with dizzying skyscrapers.

Houses of Parliament

The buildings of the parliament, seat of legislative power in South Africa, are on Government Avenue. The main building, with central dome and Corinthian columns, also houses the Library of Parliament. You can visit the buildings during the week on a guided tour. The avenue verges on the **Company Gardens**. This large shady park started life as fruit and vegetable gardens under Van Riebeeck and was later converted into a splendid botanical garden.

City Hall

To the northeast on Darling Street, City Hall is built in an architectural style at once reminiscent of the Italian Renaissance and British colonial times. This remarkable building of 1905 is used today as a concert hall and for special ceremonies. It is set off by a huge esplanade, where a lively market is held daily.

Castle of Good Hope

Built in 1666, the castle is one of the oldest European constructions in southern Africa. In the form of a five-pointed star, this fortress has never been under siege and owes its celebrity to the men of note who were imprisoned within its walls. The main attractions are the Ceremony of the Keys, which takes place at 10 a.m., and the Changing of the Guard, at noon. The guided tour includes the torture chambers and cells; it will make you wonder how they came to call the castle "Good Hope".

Museums

Most of Cape Town's museums are managed by Iziko, and are currently undergoing renovation and upgrading, including the installation of wheelchair access.

At the south end of the Company Gardens in Queen Victoria Street, the **Iziko South African Museum** was established in 1825 by Lord Charles Somerset and enjoys an international reputation, founded on the natural history department. It is worth a visit for the anthropology section and Planetarium alone. The collections range from Stone Age tools and fossils to traditional clothing and document all forms of life in Southern Africa.

Opposite, the **Iziko South African National Gallery** has a permanent collection of works by both national and international artists and includes photography, sculpture, architecture, beadwork and textiles as well as paintings.

The nearby **Jewish Museum**, on Hatfield Street in the oldest synagogue in the country, has a good collection of ceremonial art and recounts the history of the Jewish communities of the Cape.

On the corner of Government Avenue and Orange Street, the late-Georgian **Bertram House** is furnished in the style of a well-to-do English home of the 18th century. It displays a large collection of English and Chinese porcelain.

Rust en Vreugd, the 18th-century home of an official of the Dutch East India Company, displays a collection of watercolours, prints and drawings donated by the artist William Fehr in 1965.

The **District Six Museum** in Buitenkant Street hosts a moving collection of recordings and artefacts that mourn the passing of the vibrant multiracial suburb of District Six, which was razed by the apartheid government in the 1960s.

The **Slave Lodge Museum**, at the junction of Wale and Adderley streets, consists of restored slave quarters built in 1679 by the Dutch East India Company. Inside, multimedia displays chart the history of slavery and the slave trade in the Cape and further afield.

West of here, on Greenmarket Square, the **Old Town House** is the former City Hall, built in 1755 in Cape rococo style. It houses the Michaelis collection of 17th-century works by great artists of the Netherlands such as Frans Hals, Jan Steen, Jacob Ruisdal and Anthony van Dyck. Concerts and lectures are held here, as well as temporary exhibitions.

Bo-Kaap

At the foot of Signal Hill, the brightly coloured dwellings of the Bo-Kaap ("above the Cape") district are inhabited by the descendants of Malay slaves who were brought here during the Dutch occupation. It remains a staunchly Islamic community.

The earliest mosque of the Cape, the **Jamia Mosque** (1850), stands at Chiappini and Castle streets and illustrates, along with the **Bo-Kaap Museum** at 71 Wale Street, the Islamic culture of the area.

Historic Monuments

Begin with the pretty Victorian houses of **Long Street**, where antique dealers and booksellers abound and the South African Association of Arts displays the works of contemporary South African artists.

On Longmarket, the **Groote Kerk**, the country's oldest church (1704), has a wooden pulpit sculpted by Anton Anreith and a fine collection of Cape silver.

Victoria and Alfred Waterfront

Prince Alfred, son of Queen Victoria, laid the foundation stone of these basins and quays in 1860. A short distance from the city centre, the area underwent a facelift in the 1990s and is now a focal point attracting the Cape's young crowd day and night. Tourists, of course, are carried along with the throng. You can stroll, shop or enjoy a good meal at any of several dozen restaurants—fresh fish and seafood are specialities. Here, too, are museums, theatres, a brewery, hotels, luxury boutiques and a huge shopping centre. This is also the place to book boat trips and helicopter flights over the surrounding region. You can visit **SAS Somerset**, a museum ship since 1988. She was built in Tyneside in 1941 and sailed for South Africa to Saldanha Bay where, as *HM Barcross,* she laid and serviced boom defence equipment.

Beaches

The nearest beach to the city centre, **Sea Point** is a densely populated area with tall apartment buildings and hotels facing many small sandy coves. **Clifton** is more spacious and is popular with the young and fashionable, while nudists head to **Sandy Bay**.

Robben Island

North of Table Bay, 5 km (3 miles) offshore, lies the notorious former prison island where Nelson Mandela and numerous other political prisoners were held for 18 years. Fascinating but sobering 4-hour tours to the island (now a UNESCO World Heritage Site) leave several times daily from the Nelson Mandela Gateway in the Victoria and Alfred Waterfront.

Table Mountain

In fine weather, a cable car will carry you up to the top of Table Mountain in seven minutes—the hike up (safer with a guide) takes about two hours. From the sum-

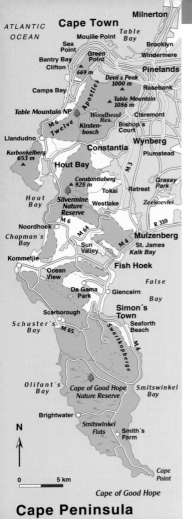

Cape Peninsula

mit, at an altitude of 1,086 m (3,570 ft), you can survey one of the finest panoramas in all South Africa—inspiration to meander among the wild flowers on one of the walks and climbs adapted to all levels of ability. Common mammals on the mountain include the rock hyrax and troops of habituated baboons. For the adventurous, abseiling excursions on a spectacular rock face near the cable car terminus can be arranged on the spot.

Southern Suburbs
In Rondebosch, on the eastern slopes of Table Mountain, the **Kirstenbosch Botanical Gardens** display 4,000 species of South African plants, including no fewer than 2,600 natives of the Cape Peninsula.

Further south in the suburb of Constantia, **Groot Constantia** is the country's oldest established vineyard. The superb 17th-century manor house in Dutch gabled style is furnished with antique pieces of the period. There is a Wine Museum in the cellar. The homestead is run by Iziko Museums of Cape Town.

Cape Peninsula
Extending 50 km (31 miles) south from Cape Town, the Cape Peninsula is a scenic feast of tree-covered mountain slopes and a dramatic coastline of soaring

cliffs, rocky bays and lagoons. The best beaches are at the northern end, with warmer waters on the east side facing False Bay. The road round the peninsula stays close to the sea wherever it can, revealing a succession of superb views. **Chapman's Peak Drive**, cut into the rock face above Hout Bay, is one of the highlights.

Hout Bay

The best harbour on the west side of the peninsula is the home of a fishing fleet. **Mariner's Wharf** on the quay is the place to buy rock lobsters (crayfish), live or ready cooked, or to dine in one of the restaurants. Artists have moved into some of the old houses and others are used as holiday homes.

Cape of Good Hope

The most southerly landfall of Africa is Cape Agulhas, 150 km (94 miles) to the southeast. But both historically and touristically, Bartolomeu Dias's Cape of Storms, renamed Good Hope by John II of Portugal, remains the focal point of an astonishing region and an obligatory pilgrimage for every visitor.

Now part of Table Mountain National Park, the Cape of Good Hope has been protected as a nature reserve since 1939, and almost 2,500 varieties of flowers bloom between and on its rocky slopes. Here you will see the del-

istockphoto.com/Freder

Penguins test the sand at Boulders Beach.

icate marsh rose, a member of the family of proteaceae that has so far resisted all attempts to cultivate it. Every spring, the Cape Peninsula celebrates the wedding of the cold waters of the Atlantic with the warm eastern seas amidst a terrestrial ocean of flowers. Surrounded by these splendours, ostrich, baboon and bontebok cavort in freedom.

Simon's Town

Once a British naval base, this port is now the headquarters of the South African Navy, whose

A line-up of beach huts on Muizenberg beach.

frigates share the harbour with countless pleasure craft. Ashore, you can see the 1740 Admiralty building. A 1790 Martello Tower houses the **Naval Museum**.

A popular nearby attraction is **Boulders Beach**, where a 3,000 strong breeding colony of penguin fusses, squawks and waddles around like an army of hysterical black-tie waiters.

Fish Hoek

With a fine safe beach for swimming, Fish Hoek on the more sheltered east side of the peninsula is a popular resort with local families and Europeans fleeing the northern winter. Until recently, the suburb was unique in South Africa in being "dry"; bars and liquor stores were banned when land was granted to build the town in the 19th century. Today, alcohol is served in restaurants and bars but there is still no bottle store.

Muizenberg

The fast inland highway from Cape Town brings city dwellers in their thousands to the holiday retreats along Muizenberg Bay, the start of an amazing 35-km (22-mile) stretch of wide sandy beach. Many people from Johannesburg have second homes here.

Hermanus

This quaint town—all cobbled alleys and creaky Victorian buildings—is an old whaling station perched dramatically below the cliffs of Walker Bay, about 80 km (50 miles) east of Cape Town as the crow flies. The cliffs form a spectacular vantage point for whale watching, most reliably from June to late October, when Southern Right Whales migrate here from Antarctica to breed.

Wine Country

The charming university town of **Stellenbosch**, founded by Simon van der Stel in 1679, is the second oldest settlement in the country, on the banks of the Eerste River about an hour's drive inland of Cape Town. Distinguished by its shady oak-lined avenues, Stellenbosch hosts what is probably the greatest concentration of Cape Dutch gabled homes in the country, a highlight being the Village Museum, a block of restored 18th-century buildings entered from Ryneveld Road.

Stellenbosch is the principal town of the Cape Winelands. Dozens of well-known vineyards, several established in the 17th century, operate in the immediate vicinity of the town, and most can be visited for impromptu tasting sessions along the renowned **Stellenbosch Wine Route**. One of the most beautiful—and highly regarded—wine estates in the region, with a memorable setting beneath tall purple crags, is **Boschendal**, centred on a stately Cape Dutch building and reached via an avenue of tall trees. A little further afield, the historic **Vergelegen Estate** near Somerset West is one of the oldest in the country, arguably the most architecturally impressive, and it also produces some superb wines.

North of Stellenbosch, **Paarl**, named for a pearl-like rock formation overlooking the town, is the headquarters of the giant KWV wine co-operative, and boasts more than its share of historic buildings.

Tulbagh, further north still, has the finest assembly of Cape Dutch houses, restored twice—before and again after an earthquake in 1969. Nearby **Ceres** is the Cape's fruit capital, surrounded by apricot, apple and pear orchards. **Worcester**'s grapes, grown within sight of winter snows, form the basis of South Africa's best brandy.

Arguably the loveliest of the vineyard villages is **Franschhoek**, or "French Corner", where French Huguenot refugees settled after fleeing religious persecution in France in 1688. Set in a magnificent green valley a short distance east of Stellenbosch, this small village hosts a clutch of great restaurants and worthwhile museum dedicated to the history of the Huguenots.

The **Robertson Valley**, whose slopes are lined with over two dozen estates, is well worth exploring. Even the more established vineyards in this region (Robertson Winery, Van Loweren, De Wets Hof) are seldom visited by large tours, so the atmosphere at tasting sessions is less production line than it is around Stellenbosch. If you're thinking of buying, the Robertson vineyards represent great value for money.

Garden Route
From the Western Cape to the Eastern, a narrow strip of land between the coast and the mountains concentrates so much variety and scenic beauty that it has become South Africa's most popular holiday destination.

Swellendam
The most significant urban punctuation along the N2 as it runs east from Cape Town towards the

Garden Route is Swellendam, founded in 1743, making it the third-oldest town in the country. A blazing fire in 1869 destroyed many of the town's older buildings, but the old **Drostdy**, built four years after the town was founded, today doubles as a local history museum and tourist information office.

The **Bontebok National Park**, only 6 km (4 miles) from the town centre, was founded in 1930 to preserve a herd of endemic bontebok, and it also protects Cape mountain zebra, red hartebeest and a good selection of birds.

Cape Agulhas

About 100 km (60 miles) south of Swellendam, Cape Agulhas is the most southerly point in Africa, a desolate stretch of rocky coastline that has claimed at least 250 ships since the 17th century. A lighthouse built in 1848 is a national monument. About an hour's drive west of Agulhas, the picturesque **Elim** is one of the most picturesque villages in South Africa, consists of a cluster of 19th century fishing cottages .

Mossel Bay

If you are coming from Cape Town, your introduction to the Garden Route will start at Mossel Bay, where the Portuguese explorer Dias came ashore in 1488. His landing is the inspiration for the local historic and maritime museum, the **Bartolomeu Dias Museum Complex**. In the park above the beach stands an ancient milkwood tree where sailors used to leave messages to be relayed by other ships. Now an official letterbox has been installed, where you can mail home cards, which will be franked "Post Office Tree".

From Mossel Bay, there are sailings to **Seal Island** where a colony of 2,000 seals lives in the middle of a bird sanctuary, principally for Cape gannets and cormorants. The small town has also become something of a focal point for adventure activities, including bungee jumping at the nearby **Gouritz Bridge**, sea kayaking, and caged dives to look for great white sharks.

George

Founded in 1811 and named after George III of England, this pleasant, leafy town is the largest settlement along the Garden Route, and the main administrative centre for the region. It lies at the base of the Outeniqua Mountains, some 20 km (12 miles) inland as the crow flies, 60 km (36 miles) east of Mossel Bay. Landmarks include **St Mark's Anglican Cathedral** (1850), and the **Garden Route Botanical Garden** on the outskirts, established in 1997 to protect and revive an area of degraded fynbos.

The **Outeniqua Choo-Tjoe** steam train formerly undertook a daily run to Knysna but now only goes as far as Mossel Bay, following flood damage to the track. The trip is well worth taking as it's the only way to see some of the most spectacular countryside of the Garden Route. At the station, an old container depot has been converted into the **Outeniqua Railway Museum** which, besides ancient locomotives, displays road transport vehicles and toy train sets.

Wilderness

On the Knysna road, Wilderness is a small and tranquil resort town set amidst the forest-fringed lakes and lagoons of the Wilderness Sector of the recently amalgamated **Garden Route National Park**. It is an enchanting spot for canoeing, rambling and bird watching, and fishermen and watersport enthusiasts like to congregate here too.

Knysna

The most attractive and hippest town along the Garden Route, Knysna was reputedly founded by George Rex, a British-born entrepreneur who settled here in 1804 and was said to be an illegitimate son of George III. Set on the shores of a lagoon, Knysna's claim to fame is the size and succulence of its oysters: oyster-and-champagne sunset cruises run

istockphoto.com/nan den Bergh

The pincushion protea attracts insects and consequently, the birds.

daily from the waterfront. It also hosts one of South Africa's pre-eminent gay events, in the form of the annual Pink Loerie Mardi Gras, which has been held in April or May every year since 2000.

Nature-lovers never fail to be impressed by the pink rocks of the **Knysna Heads**, a pair of cliffs that hem in the lagoon. The indigenous forests carpeting the slopes of the Outeniqua Mountains are famed for ancient stinkwood and yellowwood trees. These are protected in a several forest reserves as well as the Garden Route National Park, and several specimens can be seen in the Garden of Eden en route to Plettenberg Bay.

The **Diepwalle State Forest**, north of Knysna, is said to protect the last truly wild elephants in the Western Cape, which remain elusive. Adventure activities in the vicinity of Knysna—bookable through the tourist information office—include abseiling, diving, mountain bike trails, and canoeing up the river.

Plettenberg Bay

This most opulent of the Garden Route resorts boasts three pretty beaches and has a huge selection of accommodation options suited to all budgets.

The **Robberg Nature Reserve**, 10 km (6 miles) out of town, protects a craggy peninsula covered by a 10-km walking trail. Seals and humpbacked whales are occasionally seen from the cliffs of Robberg, and a variety of seabirds—notably a breeding colony of the handsome black oystercatcher—is guaranteed.

Totally different in character, the **Keurbooms River Nature Reserve**, 4 km (2.5 miles) out of town, protects a stretch of the river fringed by lush forest teeming with small mammals and birds, and best explored along an overnight canoe trail.

Tsitsikamma

Protecting an 80-km (50-mile) stretch of rugged coastline east of Plettenberg Bay, the Tsitsikamma sector of the Garden Route National Park is perhaps best-known as the site of the magnificent **Otter Trail**, which is often booked solid a year in advance. A taster of what this hike offers is provided by day walks out of the Storms River rest camp, which lies near the breathtaking cliffs that enclose the Storms River Mouth. The residential village of **Nature's Valley**, at the western edge of the sector, is surrounded by coastal forest running down to a lovely, calm beach. These forests are noted for several podocarpus conifers more than 300 years old.

Cape St Francis

Further east towards Port Elizabeth, the resort of **Oyster Bay** lies on a beautiful beach. Along the shore near Cape St Francis, sea otters can be observed; the marine nature reserve is also a refuge for seals. **Jeffrey's Bay**, scattered with shells, is a paradise for surfers. The season starts in March.

Oudtshoorn

The detour inland to Oudtshoorn, about 60 km (38 miles) to the north of George, is highly recommended. You can visit the **Cango Caves** 27 km (17 miles) further north) with their stunning stalactites and stalagmites, see a **crocodile ranch**, and spend time at an **ostrich farm**. Thanks to the 19th-century fashion craze for ostrich feathers, several farmers of the region built stately homes that became known as feather palaces. These are open to visitors, with guided tours and ostrich shows. The birds, ridden by jockeys, take part in races which you can enjoy while tucking in to a tender ostrich steak.

Karoo National Park

It is well worth extending your journey by 200 km (125 miles) further north to **Beaufort West**, in the semi-desert plain of the Western Karoo. The town has a Dutch Reformed Church in the Gothic style, a museum in the old Town Hall, an old Mission Church and Manse. But the detour is chiefly justified by the Karoo National Park, offering an explosion of flowers every spring, as well as abundant game and a chance to spot the blue crane. A unique feature of this park is a walking trail that concentrates on the region's rich variety of fossils.

West Coast

A succession of beaches and fishing harbours are strung along the coast. North of Cape Town on the West Coast, the Lobster Road leads to the holiday resort of **Strandfontein**. Birds and bird-watchers alike flock to the **West Coast National Park**, one of the biggest marshlands in the world and home to some 55,000 cormorants, sandpipers, Cape gannets, gulls, plovers and pink flamingos in summer.

There's a pleasant beach at the **Langebaan Lagoon** near Churchhaven; the busy port of **Saldanha** is known for its old thatched cottages. The nearby islands are colonized by seals, penguins and Cape gannets. The area around Langebaan often becomes a riot of colour in spring—the **Postberg Nature Reserve** hosts spectacular floral displays.

At **Lambert's Bay**, the gannet colony roosts on a peninsula close to the port, along with a small flock of resident penguins. The history of the region is recounted at the Sandveld Museum.

Inland

The vast orange groves of **Citrusdal** on the Olifants River produce 2 million crates of citrus fruit every year. The valley also produces wine. Further east, the **Cedarberg Mountains** have weathered into natural sculptures of golden sandstone. Many outdoor lovers regard this spectacular range to be the finest hiking area in South Africa. It has some wonderful rock art and wildflower displays. The **Kagga Kamma Reserve** is home to a few San people.

SHOPPING

Take a measure of African mystery, a taste of the Orient, blend with typically Western luxury and you have the recipe for shopping in South Africa — as eclectic as the population. In a word, there is something for everyone.

Keep the original invoices for items you intend to export. You can then obtain a refund of the VAT (sales tax) from customs offices at ports and airports of departure from South Africa. You may have to show the goods to the customs inspectors so don't pack them away.

Preferably before going to South Africa, and certainly before you leave, find out what imports are banned in your own country. Otherwise you may face an unpleasant surprise on your return home — having your souvenirs confiscated (not to mention a fine). Most western countries have signed the Washington convention aiming to protect endangered animal and plant species.

Gems

Diamonds are virtually synonymous with South Africa, which is one of the world's principal producers. Don't forget, however, that the finest diamonds are cut in Amsterdam and Antwerp. Their value is determined by the world market price, which is dominated by De Beers. If you buy diamond jewellery, be sure to ask for an official certificate of provenance, with a full description of each stone. There is a wide selection of semi-precious gemstones, uncut or cut and mounted.

Gold

Gold may be bought for a little less than elsewhere, but be sure that you are getting 18 carat gold, as 9 carat is widespread in shops throughout the country.

Ostrich leather

For a souvenir which is both practical and attractive, choose leather goods in ostrich skin. Characterized by its bumpy surface, ostrich skin is incredibly tough and hard-wearing. Conservationists need't worry: the skins come from ostrich farms which are mainly situated around Oudtshoorn. If you feel more daring, you can also buy plumes for your Easter bonnet or a feather boa. Briefcases, handbags, wallets, shoes, belts, even jackets and coats make welcome gifts. The finest-quality leather is exported to Italy, where it is made into elegant fashion items before being sent back to South Africa to grace the smart boutiques. There is also a wide range of goods in farmed buffalo and crocodile skin.

Traditional African Art

The numerous cultures which make up South Africa have given birth to a colourful and lively tradition of craftsmanship, perpetuated for the greater happiness of the shopping-prone tourist. What with masks, spears, shields, sculpture, paintings, pottery and multicoloured bead necklaces, the choice is staggering.

And More...

If your friends are all hoping for a small souvenir of your South African journey, bear in mind the woven mats, painted ostrich eggs, Indian spices, and protea flowers. Another idea is one of the better Cape wines, brandies or citrus-flavoured liqueurs.

A Pedi craftswoman among her beaded creations. | **Baskets made by nimble fingers.** | **Slim figurines will fit neatly into your suitcase, and leave space for a bottle of good red wine.**

istockphoto.com/Parnell

flickr.com/mickeymox

flickr.com/mickeymox

flickr.com/downeym

DINING OUT

Rich agricultural lands, a livestock tradition that includes sheep, goats, cattle and poultry, and a privileged geographical situation have brought South Africa fresh produce of the highest quality: fruit, vegetables, meat, fish and seafood.

Rich, healthy and abundant, South African cooking tends to be good, plain, unsophisticated food prepared in the American style, but with borrowings from Britain, India and Southeast Asia.

Meat

Barbecues, or *braais,* are a South African institution and constitute the favourite weekend meals for family gatherings—rather like a picnic in your own garden. Indeed, most picnic sites and camping grounds are provided with barbecue pits, so that all you need is some meat or fish and a bag of charcoal to provide the basis for a pleasant Sunday in the open air.

Some South African specialities to try are *bredie,* mutton stew flavoured with tomato sauce; *boerewors*, sausages spiced with cinnamon; and *biltong*, air-dried beef, ostrich or antelope meat, usually served as a starter. Eaten mostly around the Cape, *bobotie* is curried minced meat with onions and eggs, baked.

Seafood

Fish and shellfish of all kinds figure largely on the menus of restaurants along the East Coast and around the Cape. Absolutely delicious and affordable in price, lobster is very good value, so spoil yourself. Oysters, shrimps and mussels make their appearance on magnificent seafood platters and the staggering variety of fish will tempt you to new culinary experiences: try *kingklip*, *kabeljou* or *snoek*.

Alternatives

Most towns of any size will have several restaurants offering Asian or European cuisine to tempt your jaded palate. Durban is noted for its Indian restaurants. Johannesburg and Cape Town have a great variety of international cuisines, and fast-food restaurants are springing up everywhere.

Increased interest in traditional ways means that adventurous eaters can test their courage. At African cultural evenings you may be offered samples of local "bush tucker" such as fried locusts, termites and beetle grubs, or dried worms.

Wine

South African wines have made up for the lost time of apartheid and international boycotts, improving greatly in quality and range since the 1990s, some acquiring a world-wide reputation for excellence. They are generally labelled by grape variety, with cabernet sauvignon, merlot, shiraz and pinotage (a uniquely South African hybrid of the pinot noir and hermitage) among the most widely planted reds. Connoisseurs of Bordeaux blends will especially appreciate the excellent Meerlust Rubicon. Chardonnay, sauvignon blanc and chenin blanc are the most conspicuous dry whites.

There are some good rosés. The great variety of their soils explains the diversity of the Cape vintages.

One of the delights of South Africa is eating lunch or dinner among the vineyards and tasting the local wines on the spot.

Lunch served with a smile in a typical lodge. | **Your meal may be accompanied by a spicy chakalaka, a fiery vegetable relish.** | **Juicy and tender ostrich steak, barbecued** *à point.*

Huber/Achmann

istockphoto.com/Gruendemann

istockphoto.com/Boshoff

SPORTS

Many South Africans are fanatical about fitness. Weekends are dedicated to the outdoor life; you'll see countless runners and cyclists as well as a mass migration to the beaches.

There's a boom in adventure sports, from ballooning to bungee-jumping, river-rafting, mountaineering and horseback safaris. In spectator sports, return to world competition has proved South Africa's rugby, cricket and soccer teams to be top class.

Water Sports

The endless beaches stretching along South Africa's 3,000-km (1,900-mile) shoreline are a permanent inducement to swim and take part in all kinds of popular water sports, including windsurfing, water-skiing, scuba diving and surfing (for which the Wild Coast south of Port Edward is particularly good). But watch out for the sharks and mind the tides — swim only at beaches that are marked safe. Some beaches have lifeguards on duty. In addition, most hotels have swimming pools. Inland, canoeing and rafting are available on every navigable river or stream.

South Africans are also enthusiastic sailors. In practically every port and at most waterside leisure centres you can try your hand at sailing, whatever your degree of competence.

Fishing

Fishing is popular on the high seas and in rivers (you can obtain a licence in the nearby towns or villages). The catch is particularly abundant near Cape Town, where the Indian and Atlantic oceans meet. Deep-sea fishing expeditions are organized for tourists on a regular basis, leaving from all the big ports, principally from the Cape between January and April and from Durban between June and November along the Kwa-Zulu-Natal coast.

Walking

The Blyde River Canyon Reserve in Mpumalanga and the uKhahlamba-Drakensberg are excellent places for walking or hiking through unspoilt countryside. A network of pathways has been laid out between the most attractive sites of some national parks and circuits adapted to horse-riding or to mountain-biking are also marked.

Spectator Sports

Athletics has a large following in South Africa, and many competitions are organized both outdoors and indoors. Rugby is practically a religion among the white population, cricket of course has its enthusiasts, and the national football team put on a fair show in the 2010 FIFA World Cup, which was hosted in South Africa.

Fans of motor racing flock to the track at Kyalami, north of Johannesburg, though the South African Formula 1 Grand Prix has not been held for several years. It might be revived in Cape Town, in 2012.

Tennis

Most large hotels have their own facilities and visitors will have no difficulty in finding a court.

Golf

Such is the popularity of golf that the country sometimes gives the impression of being one immense golf course. There are almost 500 official courses and visitors are welcomed everywhere, generally at prices lower than in Europe.

Sports for everyone, whether you want to just watch, or take part yourself.

istockphoto.com/Rapideye

flickr.com/Adrian

istockphoto.com/Davies

An easy way to remember the Big Five, or to recognize the banknotes.

hemis.fr/Frilet

THE HARD FACTS

To help you plan your trip, here are some of the practical details you should know about South Africa.

Airports

The major international gateway is Johannesburg (whose O. R. Tambo Airport also serves Pretoria), but an increasing number of international carriers now fly directly to Durban and Cape Town from Europe, America and Asia. All three airports have every facility required by today's traveller, including travel and car-hire agencies and duty-free shops.

Airport buses run to city centres, and some hotels operate their own shuttles.

Climate

South Africa is, for many, practically synonymous with sunny skies, and in most parts of the country it is unusual indeed to experience persistent overcast weather. South of the equator seasons are the inverse of those in the northern hemisphere: the winter solstice (the shortest day) comes in June and the summer solstice (the longest day) in December. The main rainy season in is summer (November to April), when dramatic but short-lived afternoon thundershowers are to be expected every few days. The exception is the Western Cape, where most of the rain falls in winter (June to August). In the interior, the climate is generally drier in the west; parts of the Kalahari and Karoo are semi-desert.

Local and seasonal climatic conditions vary considerably. The Cape Town area has a temperate, Mediterranean climate, while the coast of KwaZulu-Natal and the Kruger National Park enjoy permanent sub-tropical conditions. The high plateau around Johannesburg is generally warm to hot in summer but is often surprisingly chilly at night, with temperatures dropping below zero in winter. The uKhahlamba-Drakensberg can be very cold in winter—snow falls in some areas.

Winter is a good time if you are planning a photo safari.

Clothing

Pack clothing suitable for a hot temperate climate. In summer, it is advisable to include a light sweater for cooler evenings, especially if you are visiting the mountain regions or the south of the country. In winter, a couple of heavier sweaters will probably be required. You may need a raincoat if you are visiting the Cape in winter. The usual style is relaxed and casual, with sports clothes very much in vogue, especially in the mountains and the nature reserves. If you are planning to stay in luxury hotels or dine in high-class restaurants, more formal attire will be required.

There's no need to dress up like a professional ranger when you visit a game park, but the brown or beige of the traditional safari suit has its merits. Drab colours are less likely to disturb the animals. In the open vehicles used in private parks, wear a hat, sunglasses and plenty of sunscreen. At night, long sleeves, long trousers and socks help to fend off mosquitoes. You will, of course, need comfortable shoes.

Communications

All main roads and urban centres have satellite reception for mobile phones. If you are spending a while in the country, it is probably worth loading a local SIM card into your phone—this won't cost much, and calls and text messages will work out a lot more cheaply than with a foreign SIM card. If you are dependent on land lines, look out for the green call boxes that accept phone cards; this is much cheaper than calling from your hotel room, where the charges are frequently doubled. To make an international call dial 00, then the country code (1 for Canada and US, 44 for UK), the area code and local number.

Internet cafes can be found in malls and other shopping areas, and most hotels now offer wireless internet and/or a business centre with internet access. Fax machines are widely available too.

Consulates

There are foreign consulates in Pretoria, Cape Town, Johannesburg and Durban. The local yellow pages of telephone directories list them under "Consulates and Embassies".

Driving

The main roads are excellent, and even the unsurfaced roads in national parks are usually quite smooth. Driving is on the left, as in Britain. Tolls are charged on some major roads. The general speed limit is 120 kph (75 mph) on motorways and marked sections of main roads away from towns where traffic is light. Elsewhere the limit is 100 kph (62 mph). In populated areas it is

60 kph (37 mph) unless otherwise posted. Radar traps are common and seat belts must be worn. An international driving licence is required unless your national licence carries your photograph.

Members of automobile clubs can pick up free brochures and maps at South African AA offices in the big cities on presenting their membership cards. Petrol stations are reliably open from 7 a.m. to 7 p.m., but many operate 24 hours a day. Petrol is cheap by comparison to most parts of Europe, and in many places you can pay with a credit card (or a dedicated garage card). Away from towns, they can be far apart, so it's advisable to fill up whenever you get the opportunity.

Avoid driving at night or alone. Plan routes in advance, and seek local advice about safety. In the cities, close car windows and lock doors. This makes air-conditioning essential, and it's useful too in the game parks and on dusty roads where you need to keep windows shut. Park in well-lit places, guarded if possible, and leave nothing on show.

Electricity
The current is 220/250 volts AC, 50 cycles. Plugs have three round pins. Bathroom plugs for razors, hairdryers and nickel-cadmium battery chargers have two round pins.

Emergencies
To call the police, the number is the same everywhere in South Africa: 1-0111. To call an ambulance, dial 1-0177.

Formalities
Tourists from the European Union do not in general need a visa for South Africa, but must show their return ticket. A valid passport is obligatory.

Non-resident tourists can import duty free all their personal effects, and gifts and new articles to a value of 3,000 rand. Visitors over 18 can import 200 cigarettes, 50 cigars and 250 g tobacco, 1 litre spirits (liquor), 2 litres wine, 50 ml perfume and 250 ml toilet water.

Health
Standards of hygiene are very high and there is no risk involved in drinking the tap water in your hotel or in eating fruit or vegetables, no matter where you are staying. Hospitals and medical services are of a good standard, but treatment must be paid for. In an emergency you will find a list of doctors in the telephone directory under Medical practitioners.

Avoid swimming in stagnant water (bilharzia is endemic) and be aware of the dangers of malaria in the lowveld of Mpumalanga, Zululand and Swaziland (which basically means any beach or game reserve north of Durban and east of the escarpment). Consult your doctor and start your course of anti-malarial tablets before leaving home, and carry them with you. Use insect repellent, and try not to get bitten. As for any journey abroad, it is advisable to take out a health insurance policy covering illness and accident while on holiday.

Hours

Banks generally open Monday to Friday 9 a.m. to 3.30 p.m. Some branches open also on Saturday mornings 8.30 a.m. to 11 a.m. Shops generally open Monday to Friday 8.30 a.m.–5 p.m., and on Saturdays 8.30 a.m.–12.30 p.m. Post offices are open weekdays 8.30 a.m.–4.30 p.m. and Saturdays 8 a.m.–noon.

Languages

The eleven official languages are Zulu, Xhosa, South Sotho, North Sotho, Ndebele, Venda, Tswana, Shangaan, Swazi, English and Afrikaans. English is spoken in all hotels, and as in many other parts of the world it is the main language in the tourist centres.

Media

The many daily newspapers published in English cover all the local, national and international news. The South African Broadcasting Corporation (SABC) has 24 radio channels broadcasting in 17 languages and 3 television channels in 7 languages. A fourth public channel called etv broadcasts chiefly in English, as does the cable network M-Net/DSTV.

Money

The South African unit of currency is the rand (R), which is subdivided into 100 cents. Banknotes are issued in denominations of 10, 20, 50, 100 and 200 rand, and coins are 5, 10, 20 and 50 cents as well as 1, 2 and 5 rand. Note that many shops refuse R200 notes due to the high incidence of forgeries.

Visa, MasterCard and to a lesser extent American Express credit and debit cards are accepted in most hotels, restaurants and shops, Until recently, cards could not be used to pay for petrol or other fuel; this is gradually changing but many filling stations still accept cash (or dedicated garage cards) only.

Cash machines (ATMs) outside banks will generally issue cash against most internationally recognized credit cards, but beware of pickpockets and muggers who watch these sites.

Public Holidays

When a public holiday falls on a Sunday, the Monday is taken off. These are the official public holidays:

January 1	*New Year's Day*
March 21	*Human Rights*
March/April	*Good Friday and Easter Monday*
April 27	*Freedom Day*
May 1	*Workers' Day*
June 16	*Youth Day*
August 9	*National Women's Day*
September 24	*Heritage Day*
December 16	*Day of Reconciliation*
December 25	*Christmas Day*
December 26	*Day of Goodwill*

Public Transport

The best way to cover the vast distances in South Africa is by air. Several airlines serve the principal towns and cities. The railway network offers moderately priced travel in sleeping cars to most parts of the country. There are also several long-distance coach companies. An excellent hop-on, hop-off minibus service called the Baz Bus, which connects Johannesburg to Cape Town via Swaziland, KwaZulu-Natal and the Eastern Cape, is used extensively by most backpackers.

Taxis must be ordered by telephone or hired from pick-up points. Insist on having the meter switched on; if there isn't one, agree a price in advance.

Safety

By staying alert and taking sensible precautions, you should be able to avoid problems. When going out in the cities at night, travel in a group, and take a taxi to and from the restaurant, theatre or wherever you are spending the evening. Do not walk alone at night, or at any time in less-frequented places, including beaches. Don't wear or carry valuables, expensive watches or "real" jewellery. Use the security devices on hotel doors. Leave no property unattended.

Time

UTC/GMT + 2 all year round.

Tipping

Restaurant bills do not include a service charge. Tip about 10 per cent of the total bill. Porters and taxi drivers also expect a tip.

Toilets

Cleanliness—sometimes even luxury—is guaranteed in all large hotels and restaurants. Most public toilets maintain an acceptable standard.

Tourist Information

The official website of the South African Tourism Board (www.southafrica.net) is your best starting point, supplying details of all tourist offices outside the country. There are also good local tourist information offices in most significant towns and other places of interest.

A Swazi woman playing the *makhoyane*, a bowed instrument with gourd resonator.

Ariadne van Zandbergen

SWAZILAND

Enclosed on three sides by South Africa, and bordering Mozambique to the east, the Kingdom of Swaziland is one of Africa's smallest nations—about the size of Wales—and its only surviving absolute monarchy.

The nation and its people are named after the 19th-century king Mswati II.

Strong economic ties to South Africa—epitomized by an interchangeable currency and the ubiquitous South African chain stores—might sometimes lead one to think of Swaziland as a tenth province of that country in all but name. Yet, you only have to scratch beneath the surface to discover it has a quite distinctive character, determined by the cultural resilience of its rural inhabitants and their proud adherence to traditional ways. About three-quarters of the population of 1.2 million are employed in subsistence farming.

Seldom visited as a stand-alone travel destination, Swaziland forms a natural extension to a tour through South Africa—indeed, for anyone driving between the popular Kruger National Park and KwaZulu-Natal, it will be easier and more rewarding to traverse the kingdom than to pass around it. The Swazi, as a rule, are charming hosts, and scenically, the kingdom is magnificent, with the misty mountain landscapes of the western escarpment standing in compelling contrast to the sweltering acacia bush of the Mozambique border region.

Tourists generally restrict their time in Swaziland to a quick flit through, punctuated perhaps by an overnight stop. But a burgeoning selection of new sites and activities justifies a longer stay. Swazi cultural villages offer fascinating insight into traditional African lifestyles, while a clutch of low-key game reserves is noteworthy for providing the rare opportunity to track the highly endangered rhinoceros on foot. Adventure activities, too, have become a Swaziland trademark, ranging from horseback safaris and self-guided game walks to white-water rafting, abseiling and rock climbing.

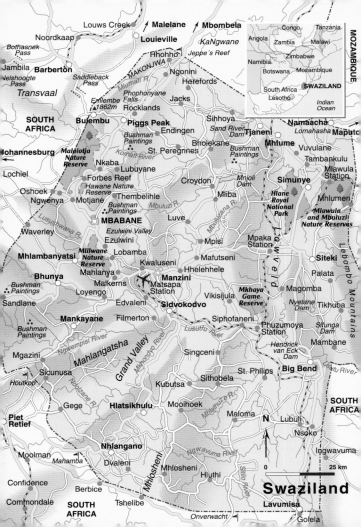

A BRIEF HISTORY

Pre-1800
Swaziland's history is similar to that of South Africa. In 1750, King Ngwane, regarded as founder of Swazi Nation, arrives in the area.

19th century
Centralization under King Sobhuza I, whose army, forged in defence against the militant Zulu, conquers an area twice as large as modern Swaziland. Outsiders call this kingdom Swazi, a corruption of the name of Sobhuza's successor Mswati II. From 1850, the Swazi regularly side with settlers against rival Zulu and Pedi, in the process being persuaded to sign one-sided treaties sacrificing parts of the kingdom for vain promises of protection. In 1894, with tacit British approval, Kruger's Transvaal Republic claims protectorateship over Swaziland. The incumbent King Bhunu doesn't accept Boer presence, and his power is reduced to such an extent that he is tried for murder.

20th century– present
Boer rule is terminated in 1902 during the aftermath of the Anglo-Boer War, when Swaziland becomes a British protectorate separately administered from South Africa. King Sobhuza II (rules 1921–82) places continual pressure on the British government to accord greater rights to his subjects, resulting in about half of the protectorate being designated as communal Swazi land in 1944. Sobhuza peacefully leads his nation to independence in 1968. Shortly afterwards, he revokes the Westminster style constitution in favour of a more traditional one—effectively outlawing opposition parties and granting the king almost absolute power. In 1986, Mswati III ascends the Swazi throne. He remains there today, albeit in an atmosphere of growing dissent against the power invested in the monarchy. A new constitution comes into effect in 2005.

Golden Jubilee of KING SOBHUZA II

SWAZIL

Carrying wood and baby the traditional way, on a batik painting.

SIGHTSEEING

Coming from the Kruger Park, the normal point of entry is the Jeppe's Reef/Matsamo border, where it's well worth stopping at the Matsamo Cultural Village in the no-man's land between immigration offices. In addition to a great coffee shop overlooking a pond stocked with crocodiles, Matsamo offers informative guided tours through a Swazi village, traditional dancing, and visits to a *sangoma* (traditional healer).

Northern Highlands

Set in rolling hills 40 km (25 miles) south of the border, the sleepy former mining town of **Piggs Peak** (founded 1884 by William Pigg) boasts a few banks and supermarkets, but is of little inherent interest to visitors. However, 10 km (6 miles) back along the Matsamo road lies the popular Piggs Peak casino, as well as the attractive **Phophonyane Falls Nature Reserve**. Privately owned and serviced by a cluster of chalets, this compact reserve is centred on an impressive waterfall, while a network of foot trails through its wooded slopes offers an opportunity to see several small mammals and a selection of colourful forest birds.

South of Piggs Peak, **Malolotja Nature Reserve** is the most beautiful sanctuary in Swaziland, protect- ing a vast landscape of hills and valleys spanning an altitude range of 640–1,829 m (2,100–6,000 ft). Some big game is present, most visibly zebra, red hartebeest and blesbok, but Malolotja is of greater interest for its unusual flora—endemic species of cycad, protea and aloe—and as a breeding site for the rare bald ibis and blue swallow. A limited road network exists, but essentially Malolotja is the domain of pedestrians: a steep but scenic half-day round hike leads to the 90-m (295-ft) **Majolomba Falls** (the tallest in Swaziland), and overnight trails of up to five nights in duration are also available.

South of the entrance gate to Malolotja, the road from **Matsamo** connects with the main road between Mbabane and the Oshoek/Ngwenya border post (the normal point of entry coming from Gauteng). Two very different sites of interest lie close to the road between the junction and the border. The **Ngwenya Glass Factory** is a unique set-up that makes and sells a wide selection of artefacts — glasses, candleholders and miniature animals — using recycled glass. More enduring in nature is **Ngwenya Mine** (a southern extension of Malolotja), the oldest known working in the world, dated to 41,000 BC, when its haematite and specularite deposits were used for ritual and decorative purposes.

The West

Sprawling over a pretty green valley in the western highlands, **Mbabane**, the national capital, with a population of about 70,000, has a rather provincial atmosphere, and — shopping malls and a few consulates aside — there's little to distinguish it from a hundred other medium-sized Southern African towns. Mbabane's temperate climate made it attractive to British settlers and it became capital of the protectorate in 1903. Contemporary photographs indicate that it then consisted of about a dozen stone buildings. A pretty Cape Dutch building on Allister Miller Street was the first British administrative office.

A short drive north of Mbabane leads to the steep, smooth slopes of **Sibebe Rock**, reputedly the largest exposed granite dome in the world, the tip of a solid chunk of granite (or batholith) that extends 15 km (9 miles) below the earth's surface. Reminiscent of Australia's famous Ayers Rock — which is larger, but composed of sandstone — Sibebe can be ascended over a couple of hours in the company of an experienced local guide.

A spectacular — and in misty conditions treacherous — asphalt road winds southwest from Mbabane through the wooded **Ezulwini Valley**, the hub of Swaziland's tourist industry. The valley is serviced by several plush hotels, many of which started life in the apartheid era, when Swaziland attracted white South Africans eager to indulge in activities that were illegal at home, such as gambling and liaising with black prostitutes. A vibrant nightlife remains a feature of the valley, and some hotels still double as casinos or strip clubs, but the main focus today is a selection of more wholesome natural and cultural sites.

The indigenous scrub of the **Mantenga Nature Reserve**, situated in the heart of the valley, supports a riot of colourful birds, while monkeys frequent the woodland near a pretty waterfall. The centrepiece is a cultural village where visitors can watch vibrant dancing displays accompanied by virtuoso traditional musicians. The village is overlooked by the **Execution Rock**—from where, in pre-colonial times, convicted murderers were thrown to their death. At the turn-off to Mantenga, Swazi Trails operates a range of adventure activities out of Ezulwini, most popularly white-water rafting trips on a nearby stretch of the **Great Usutu River** studded with Grade I–IV rapids.

Lobamba, at the south of Ezulwini Valley, is the traditional seat of the Swazi monarchy, and the site of national parliament. The informative National Museum of Swaziland at Lobamba houses several displays relating to the royal lineage, a fascinating collection of photographs from the early 19th century, and a more prosaic natural history room full of musty stuffed animals. The adjacent King Sobhuza II Memorial Park pays tribute to the popular ruler who secured Swaziland's independence from Britain, and is where his body was laid in state prior to a traditional burial in the hills.

Also in the Ezulwini Valley, **Mlilwane Nature Reserve** is the kingdom's oldest sanctuary, converted from private farmland and donated to a non-profit trust in 1969. Ecologically compromised by several stands of exotic eucalyptus, Mlilwane has nevertheless made a vital contribution to conservation in Swaziland. Hippopotamus wallow in a pool at the rest camp, while reintroduced zebra, warthog and antelope—including blue wildebeest, nyala, blesbok and impala—are common. A noteworthy feature of Mlilwane is that you can walk unguided along an extensive network of foot trails, or explore on horseback.

Roughly 40 km (25 miles) southeast of Mbabane, the road through Ezulwini emerges at **Manzini**, the kingdom's largest town and industrial hub. Founded in 1889 as Bremersdorp, Manzini served as the capital of Swaziland before being usurped by Mbabane. Although not overly endowed with character, it is of interest for its bustling central market—an excellent place to buy traditional handicrafts—and on Thursday host to a macabre traditional medicine market.

The Lowveld

Climatically and scenically, eastern Swaziland resembles bordering low-lying parts of Mpumalanga and KwaZulu-Natal, and it supports several vast sugar plantations around Simunye and Big Bend. The country's main concentration of game reserves also lies in the eastern lowveld, and while none exists on the scale of the Kruger Park, all are worth exploring. Swaziland's wildlife showpiece is **Hlane Royal National Park**, a 3,000-ha tract of bush originally set aside as the royal hunting ground, and still visited on ceremonial occasions by King Mswati III to pot an antelope. The rest camp at the entrance gate overlooks a waterhole that attracts a steady trickle of game. Self-drive roads offer perhaps the highest probability in Southern Africa of spotting white rhino, while elephant, black rhino, greater kudu and nyala are regularly seen. Lions and cheetahs are housed in large natural enclosures that can be visited only with escorted trips in four-wheel drive vehicles arranged at the rest camp. Inexpensive guided walks run through an area teeming with rhinos and elephants.

East of Hlane, a trio of contiguous reserves protects the lushly wooded slopes of the Lubombo Mountains and associated river valleys. **Mbuluzi** and **Mlawula Nature Reserves** protect giraffe, zebra, various antelope, and an excellent range of birds, and since no dangerous large mammals are present, they can be explored on foot. By contrast, **Shewula Mountain Camp**, unique within Swaziland in that it's owned and managed by a local community, is primarily a cultural centre: local village visits and other cultural activities are run out of a clifftop rest camp offering spectacular views in three directions.

Further south, the dense acacia woodland of **Mkhaya Game Reserve** was set aside in 1979 to protect Swaziland's last surviving herd of pure Nguni cattle, a breed with high resistance to diseases that can kill exotic caws. Mkhaya also hosts introduced breeding herds of locally endangered game species such as sable and roan antelope. Dense populations of both Africa's rhino species, as well as elephant, are easily observed. Mkhaya is too small to support large predators without a risk of them attacking local livestock, but leopard spoor is occasionally seen.

Shopping

Many curios and handicrafts sold in South Africa are imported from Swaziland, and it's cheaper—and healthier for the local economy—to buy at source. The glass factory at Ngwenya is well worth a visit, as is the renowned candle factory in the Ezulwini Valley. The produce of both can be bought at curio shops and stalls all countrywide, as can a wide selection of Swazi basketry, beadwork and carvings.

Well-stocked supermarkets are found in all major centres, but the selection of goods in smaller towns is limited.

PRACTICAL INFORMATION

In most respects, what is true for South Africa holds true for Swaziland. Exceptions are noted below.

Credit cards. Most hotels, restaurants and larger shops accept credit cards, but ATMs issuing cash against credit cards exist only in Piggs Peak, Ezulwini, Mbabane and Manzini.

Currency. The Swazi *Lilangeni* (plural *Emalangeni*) is pegged to the South African Rand. The two currencies are interchangeable within Swaziland, but not within South Africa—so don't leave Swaziland with excess *Emalangeni*.

Driving. South African vehicles entering Swaziland must pay a nominal insurance fee at the border. Be wary of animals and pedestrians running unexpectedly into the road.

Language. The official languages are Swazi and English, the latter generally spoken to a high standard.

A hard climb to the top of the dunes in
Namib Naukluft Park.

Hübe/ Wnau

NAMIBIA

From magnificent red-gold sand dunes to a diamond-studded mineral bonanza land, from the gloomily named Skeleton Coast to the time-warped architecture of the towns, Africa's youngest independent country is clearly somewhere very different. Etosha, its greatest national park, is home to elephants and lions.

Namibia has only been independent since 1990. Before that it was ruled from South Africa, but for three decades at the turn of the 20th century it was a German colony. The Kaiser's era left a lasting mark on the urban landscape — and on the gastronomic traditions, which still incline towards sausages and sauerkraut and plenty of beer. Karneval and Oktoberfest are the year's biggest festivals at Windhoek, the colourful upland capital.

Sparsely populated, Namibia is about three-quarters the area of South Africa, or ten times the size of Austria. It is bordered on the west by the South Atlantic, on the south by South Africa, on the east by Botswana and on the north, Angola. And a bit of gerrymandering, the narrow panhandle of the Caprivi Strip, extends Namibia's frontier like a barbed spear into Zambia and to the tip of Zimbabwe.

In the rainbow of races united under the blue, green, red and gold Namibian flag, members of tribes linked under the Ovambo name account for about half the population of 2 million. The Kabango, Herero and Damara people come next, and white Namibians are estimated to total 120,000. The population of handsome hunter-gatherer Bushmen, or San, has dwindled to a few tens of thousands. About 90 percent of all Namibians profess Christianity, with the Lutherans easily in first place.

The treacherous coast stretches for about 1,500 km (more than 900 miles), yet there is only one proper deepwater port, Walvis Bay, long a strategic enclave of South Africa. The highway network is in good shape. Inland there is still plenty of room for antelope and zebra, giraffe and hippo, and sights that can only be seen in the heart of Africa.

Namibia

ANGOLA

Ludango

ANGOLA

Popa
Falls
Mahango
Game Park

Caprivi
Game
Park

Katima
Mulilo

Kongola

Mudumu
National
Park

ZAM

NAMIBIA

Mamili
National
Park

BOTSWA

Cunene

Okavango

Ruacana

Owambo Country

Rundu

Kunene

Oshakati

Ondangwa

Kaudo
Game P

Opuwo

Tsintsabis

Etosha National
Park

Etosha Pan

Namutoni

Omaramba Omatako

Sesfontein

Okaukuejo

Halali

Tsumeb

Grootfontein

Tsumkwe

Hoba
Meteorite

Kamanjab

Otavi

Skeleton Coast Park

Damaraland

Dolomite
Caves

Outjo

Ugab

Otjozondjup
Region

Terrace Bay

Palm

Petrified
Forest

Khoixas

Rock Finger

Otjiwarongo

Waterberg Plateau
Park

Okakarara

Torra Bay

Twyfelfontein

Burnt
Mountain

Kalkfeld

Otjinene

Brandberg
2573m

The White
Lady

Dinosaur
Footprints

Hochfeld

Summerdown

ATLANTIC
OCEAN

Messum
Crater

Ulis

Omaruru

Spitzkoppe
1829m

Erongo Mts
2318m

Cape Cross
(Seal Reserve)

Henties Bay

Usakos

Okahandja
Von Bach Dam

Steinhausen

Karibib

Gross Barmen

Omitara

Buitepos

Swakopmund

Daan Viljoen
Game Park

WINDHOEK

Witvlei

Gobabis

Walvis Bay

Bird
Paradise

Leonardville

B
O
T
S
W
A
N
A

Tropic of Capricorn

Rehoboth

Uhlenhorst

Aminus

Kuiseb

Solitaire

Aranos

Namib Naukluft Park

Hardap
Recreation
Resort

Stampriet

Akanous

Maltahöhe

Mariental

Gochas

Kgal
Transf
N

Namib Desert

Sossusvlei

Gibeon
Station

Witbooisvlei

Twee Rivier

Brukkaros

Helmeringhausen

Tses

Köes

Kokerboom
Forest

Bethanie

AFRICA

Lüderitz

Aus

Goageb

Seeheim

Keetmanshoop

Aroab

Ariamsvle

NAMIBIA

Kolmanskop

Narubis

Stone
Rondavel

Fish

Elizabeth
Bay

Rock Engravings
Music Stones

Fish River
Canyon

Grünau

Diamond Area

Rosh Pinah

Ai-Ais

Karasburg

Sperrgebiet
NP

Warmbad

N

Noordoewer

SOUT

Namibia

0   100 km

Oranjemund

Orange

Cape Town

AFRIC

A BRIEF HISTORY

Prehistory
The early inhabitants are thought to have been Khoisan speakers, including San (Bushmen) and Khoikhoi, or Nama, people.

15th century
Portuguese explorer Diego Cão marks his visit to Cape Cross by erecting a cross on the shore. His countryman, Bartolomeu Diaz, "discovers" Walvis Bay, but finding no fresh water he abandons thoughts of colonization.

18th century
In 1793 the Dutch claim Walvis Bay. But Britain soon annexes South Africa's Cape Colony (1795) and claims the adjoining Namibian coast.

19th century
First German missionary station opened at Bethanie in 1814. The missionaries fan out through the territory in mid-century. They ask Britain for protection but this is refused. Britain annexes Walvis Bay in 1878. A Bremen merchant, Adolf Lüderitz, buys the small port of Angra Pequena in 1883 and raises the German flag over what is to become the town of Lüderitz. In the 1880s and 1890s German settlers occupy other parts of what they call South West Africa, signing treaties with native tribes. Swakopmund is founded in 1893 by Captain Curt von François and 120 German colonial troops. At the turn of the 20th century Herero tribesmen and Germans engage in years of bloody battles. The well-armed Germans win.

20th century–present
In 1908, Germans discover the world's richest diamond bonanza in the southern zone of South West Africa; prospectors flood in. During World War I, on behalf of the Allies, South African forces capture South West Africa from Germany. "Undesirable" German settlers and military personnel are expelled. South Africa rules under a 1920 League of Nations mandate. When the United Nations succeeds the League of Nations after World War II, South Africa refuses to put South West Africa under UN trusteeship. The South West African People's Organization (Swapo) is established in 1958 and in 1966 launches a guerrilla war for independence. After UN-supervised elections, Namibia becomes an independent nation in 1990. Its first president is Sam Nujoma, leader of Swapo. In 1993 South Africa hands over Walvis Bay sovereignty to Namibia. Nujoma's chosen successor Hifikepunye Pohamba becomes president in March 2005 and is re-elected in 2009.

A Herero lady watches the world passing by her house in Swakopmund.

SIGHTSEEING

The tourist authorities divide Namibia into four regions: Northern, Central, Southern and Namib. These are arbitrary delineations that have nothing to do with provincial boundaries or other formalities. For practical reasons this guide follows the same format, beginning the tour in the central highlands, site of the nation's capital.

Windhoek

The compact skyscrapers of Windhoek oversee a prosperous and individualistic city of more than 300,000 residents, roughly 15 per cent of the national population. The Germans who made this their colonial capital more than a century ago left their European imprint on Africa, a quaint legacy of Old World architecture, landscaping and lifestyle.

At an elevation of 1,650 m (5,400 ft), the capital is largely immune to the swelter you might expect of Africa. Although the name literally means "windy corner", Windhoek has few blustery problems; the climate is refreshing with plenty of rain to keep the lush gardens and flowerbeds well watered.

As dynamic as the skyscrapers may be, it's the low-rise monuments from colonial days that win on charm. Start with the **Alte Feste**, an old whitewashed fort designed by Curt von François in 1890. Its severity is relieved by palm trees and gardens. The oldest structure in town now houses part of the **National Museum of Namibia**, dealing with aspects of the country's history and culture from tribal times to independence.

The **Parliament** building, dating from late in the German era, owes its curious nickname of Tintenpalast (Ink Palace) to the reams of edicts and reports penned by the bureaucrats on duty inside.

The **Christuskirche** (Church of Christ) was built during the same period as the Tintenpalast, in the first decade of the 20th century, to offer thanks for the end of wars between the Germans and local tribes. This Evangelical Lutheran church, a red-roofed Gothic Revival building in native quartz sandstone and Italian marble rises gracefully to the tip of its slender

Windhoek's Christuskirche was dedicated as the Church of Peace.

istockphoto.com/Richter

Central Excursions

Local colour, charm and cleanliness commend Windhoek to the visitor. The capital is also a good base for excursions into the hinterland. For instance, less than half an hour's drive takes you to the **Daan Viljoen Game Park** (privatized in 2010), where you can start your checklist of African wild animals. You'll get close to highland game animals like springbok and Hartmann's mountain zebra, hartebeest and eland (Africa's largest antelope). There are no lions or other dangerous animals so the park is a safe place to travel on foot; just follow the marked trails. And the bird-watching is first class.

The **Von Bach Dam and Recreation Resort**, in the mountains north of Windhoek, is a favourite getaway spot for the capital's sportsmen, especially anglers. The dam positively wriggles with carp, bream and black bass.

The highway and the railway line for the coast veer west at the attractive and historic town of **Okahandja**, the old capital of the Hereros, about 70 km (40 miles) north of Windhoek. Every year (in August) crowds of colourfully dressed participants gather for a memorial service to honour the Herero chiefs buried here. And here, too, is the tomb of Chief Jonker Afrikaner, originally an arch-foe of the Hereros. The

clock tower. The lead-glass windows were a gift from Kaiser Wilhelm II.

The architecture on the main street, **Independence Avenue** (formerly Kaiserstrasse), is a lively contrast between the steep, overhanging red roofs of the Germanic tradition and new international-style high rises. Strolling and shopping are rewarding. Take a break at an outdoor café, where the beer, too, recalls old Germany, but the passers-by represent a brilliant medley of European and African cultures.

town's church, now a national monument, was built in the 1870s, after the foundation of a mission station.

Just southwest of Okahandja, Namibians and foreigners "take the waters" in a luxurious hot spring resort on the site of a historic mission station. It's called **Gross-Barmen**, based on the name of the town the German missionaries came from in the 1840s. The ruins of the mission and an army camp remain. The natural springs here produce water rich in fluorides and sulphides, which bubbles out of the ground too hot to bathe in. It has to be cooled for use in the thermal baths and further cooled for the outdoor swimming pool, which is not exactly chilly, either.

The junction town of **Karibib**, west of Okahandja, owes its prosperity to the railway, a mission station and, last but not least, a nearby gold mine. The earth is truly generous here: fine marble of international renown is quarried in the area, and there are reserves of gemstones.

Omaruru, on the way to the Etosha National Park, has a violent history. The Germans established a police post here, and it was besieged by the Hereros in a brutal war in 1904, with heavy losses. A museum documents the Herero War and the tragic battle of Omaruru.

Mountain scenery and Stone Age culture are the attractions of the **Erongo Mountains**. The best-known site is **Phillip's Cave**, in which a white Stone Age wall-painting of an elephant shows remarkable detail.

More rock paintings are found near the **Spitzkoppe**, a family of granite peaks (advertised as the "Matterhorn of Namibia") rising suddenly from the plain. Because of the setting the mountains appear taller than they really are (around 1,800 m or 5,900 ft).

North of Omaruru, the railway tracks go through the village of Kalkfeld, but what makes the area famous are **dinosaur tracks**. The footprints, thought to be more than 150 million years old, are now a national monument.

The next stop on the railway is the junction town of **Otjiwarongo**, a prosperous market centre. The main attraction in this area is the AfriCat Foundation, which has played an important part in the capture, rehabilitation and re-release into the wild of Namibia's big cats, particularly cheetah, which naturally thrive in this open habitat but are frequently persecuted by livestock farmers.

For a change of scenery and altitude, you can see some fascinating game roaming **Waterberg Plateau Park**. This national park encompasses most of the fertile, flat top of a mountain rising dramatically east of Otjiwarongo. Endangered species were given priority in populating the surprisingly lush landscape. Among those prospering here are white and black rhino, roan and sable antelope, giraffe, cheetah, and a highly prized colony of rare Cape vultures. The Waterberg is also known for its rock paintings and engravings.

Unusual geological sights are a speciality of the **Damaraland** region, west of Otjiwarongo. Looking as tall as a skyscraper, **Vingerklip** ("rock finger") is an odd outcrop, a limestone monolith left over from centuries of erosion, standing 35 m (115 ft) high.

Fossils of tree trunks thought to be 200 million years old and amazingly well-preserved are the phenomenon of the **Petrified Forest**, a national monument near Khorixas. Geologists believe the trees were uprooted elsewhere and carried here by floodwaters about 250 million years ago.

Twyfelfontein was listed as Namibia's first UNESCO World Heritage Site in 2007. The site hosts one of Africa's greatest concentrations of rock petroglyphs. Thousands of paintings and engravings deal with the concerns of the Stone Age hunter-gatherers who lived here 6,000 years ago — lions, giraffes, elephants and rhinos. Later rock art was done by Khoikhoi herders 2,000 years ago.

And one more geological wonder: near the **Burnt Mountain** (a study in desolation), slabs of basalt stand like a surreal skyscraper skyline. They are called the **Organ Pipes** and are probably more than 100 million years old.

The South

The pleasant town known as the "capital of the south", **Keetmanshoop**, was founded by German missionaries in the 1860s. The former Rhenish mission church, built in 1895, houses a museum of colonial memories and ethnological exhibits. Farmers in the Keetmanshoop area raise karakul sheep for their wool and fur (known in some circles as Persian lamb, but the Namibian variant is called Swakara). The dry, hot climate here agrees with the animals, natives of Central Asia.

The arid land just northeast of Keetmanshoop also supports hundreds of strange botanical specimens in the **Kokerboom Forest**. Also called quiver trees, they are not trees at all, but giant aloes resembling parched, peeling dragon trees. They grow to a height of 8 m (more than 25 ft).

Namibia's version of the Grand Canyon, the **Fish River Canyon**, is a ravine that is up to 27 km (17 miles) wide and in places more than 500 m (1,600ft) deep. At the bottom of this spectacular gorge, the river itself is a bit of an anticlimax — a trickle at best, except at flood time.

Ai-Ais (the name means scalding hot) is a spa in the wilderness of the canyon. You'll find the hot springs at the heart of a thoroughly modern resort complex with facilities for all sorts of therapeutic endeavours as well as rest and recreation.

For history buffs the village of **Bethanie** holds a certain appeal. This is where the German colonial powers, represented by Adolf Lüderitz, signed the first treaty with the Hottentots in the house of Nama chief Josef Frederiks. In Bethanie stands the country's oldest European house (1814), a one-room cottage called Schmelenhaus after the missionary Heinrich Schmelen. Bethanie was founded by the London Missionary Society but they were short of recruits and sent a German instead. The Schmelenhaus is a national monument and museum. The original church built in 1859 is still standing.

Namib Region

The sleepy town of **Lüderitz** was the first German port in South West Africa, but its history can be traced back to a visit by the 15th-

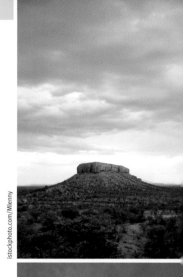

Table Mountain in the Damaraland region. | The branches of the kokerboom were used to make quivers.

century Portuguese explorer Bartolomeu Diaz. The fanciful German architecture from the first decade of the 20th century adds charm to the romantic setting.

The **Namib-Naukluft Park,** Namibia's biggest national park, encompasses a staggering array of scenery, from mountains to grasslands to a desert of titanic dunes. The animal inhabitants are just as varied — gemsbok (oryx), Hartmann's mountain zebra, springbok, ostriches, and raptors such as eagles and falcons. The park covers an area of nearly 50,000 sq km (more than 19,000 sq miles), the size of New Hampshire and Vermont together, or Sicily plus Sardinia. The desert reaches the most impressive dimensions in the central Sossusvlei area, reputed to have the tallest sand dunes in the world —

piled up to heights of 300 m (nearly 1,000 ft). The desert supports more life than you may imagine: grasses, succulents and a unique prehistoric plant called *Welwitschia mirabilis*, which takes its moisture from the fog or dew.

Walvis Bay, the only deepwater port between Cape Town and Angola, is a working port where freighters load up with Namibian minerals and trawlers feed the fish-processing factories. The production of sea salt accounts for blinding white hills around the lagoon, made up of crystals evolving through evaporation.

Birdwatchers haunt the lagoon here and at nearby **Sandwich Harbour** for the spectacle of thousands of flamingos and droves of other species, both permanent residents and transients, thriving on the abundant seafood. Sea birds nest on giant "bird islands" offshore, built to exploit the value of their guano, which is exported most profitably as fertilizer.

The C14 highway heading inland from Walvis Bay soon enters the desert, providing a panorama of rolling dunes. Sliding down a steep sand hill is the sort of sport most visitors won't soon forget.

Holidaymakers come to **Swakopmund**, across the river north of Walvis Bay. They savour its charm, its mild climate and attractive beach. This is a corner of old Germany on the South Atlantic, rich in architectural and other memories of the late 19th century when Captain von François and Dr Heinrich Göring (who would father the future Reichsmarschall) attempted to put an end to tribal wars and build a colony.

Typical of the transplanted European atmosphere of the town, the former railway station (built in 1901) is solid and stately, with a steeple and verandas, and palm trees to make it all seem out of joint. It has been refurbished as an elegant hotel in colonial style.

Other distinguished buildings of the era are scattered through the town: the Old District Courthouse, an Art Nouveau classic; the old gabled prison; and mansions like Woermann House, now serving as the public library, and Rittenburg, and the Hohenzollern House. There is also a sparkling modern Crystal Gallery.

Near the beach, the Swakopmund Museum occupies the former Customs House. There are exhibits on the various indigenous cultures—weapons, artefacts, musical instruments and tools—as well as desert and ocean themes.

Visitors are often taken to admire a marvel of Industrial Revolution days, an 1896 steam locomotive nicknamed *Martin Luther*. The name is a wry reference

Direct current. An oceanographic phenomenon, the Benguela Current takes the credit or blame for almost everything along the Namibian coast, from the wealth of fish to the prevalence of fog in autumn, winter and spring. Carrying some of the chill of Antarctica, the current causes rainfall to condense before it can go ashore, but the fog helps to make the desert bloom and provides drinking water for creatures large and small. The cold ocean also moderates the heat that would otherwise roast the countryside at these latitudes.

istockphoto.com/Parsons

to the engine's career—it was mostly broken down—and Luther's statement, "Here I stand…"

You don't have to go far out of town to experience the **Namib desert** (for which the region and the country are named). Some of it is the dune of your dreams, but much is a less glamorous rocky expanse. Here, too, is **Rössing**, a rare site for connoisseurs of industrial superlatives. This is said to be the largest open-cast uranium mine in the world, and visitors can watch the mechanical behemoths collecting the ore from this awesome hole in the ground.

Cape Cross, up the coast from Swakopmund, is the place where the first European explorer came ashore in these parts, and here Diego Cão planted a cross. Now the area is a seal reserve, the home of tens of thousands of Cape fur seals.

The **Skeleton Coast** has had its share of shipwrecks and other disasters, which gave rise to the forbidding name. The landscape is as varied as hypnotic dunes, rugged mountains and, of course, a beach that seems to go on to infinity. Anglers land fish of inspiring proportions—blacktail, galjoen, kob and, perhaps less appealingly, shark.

Because of the hostile climate and terrain, the wildlife population ashore is rather skimpy, mostly antelope, jackal and ostrich. And rarest of all nowadays, the desert lion.

The North

In Namibia's wonderful **Etosha National Park**, you can see lions, black rhino, elephants, giraffe, zebra and antelopes of many families. What brings the animals here is the Etosha Pan, a huge depression that is sometimes filled with rainwater. But around its periphery are springs that provide year-round refreshment for throngs of animals and birds. The mineral-rich springs also feed the grass, shrubs and trees in which the game like to hide.

Among the more gripping sights you may come across as you drive through the park: hyena, wildebeest, scaly anteater, and antelope including kudu, duiker, eland, gemsbok, and the tiny Damara dik-dik. Bird-watchers can try to chalk up some 325 species as spectacular as the lilac-breasted roller and the crimson-breasted shrike.

The area of the park has shrunk and expanded over the years, sometimes controversially, as the interests of farmers competed with wildlife preservation efforts. At last report Etosha covered 22,270 sq km (nearly 8,600 sq miles), which is bigger than Massachusetts, or more than half as large as Denmark.

Namutoni, near the eastern edge of the park, was the site of a small fort at the turn of the 20th century. A successor fort, long a ruin, was restored to its "Beau Geste" silhouette, declared a national monument, and turned into tourist accommodation. **Okaukuejo**, the administrative headquarters, has many tourist comforts and some truly dramatic entertainment: a floodlit waterhole where game can be admired at night. The third camp, **Halali**, with modern facilities, is located between the other two. All of them are open year-round.

East of the park, **Tsumeb** is a pleasantly shaded mining town, thriving on the basis of more than 184 different minerals found here. In addition to the minerals valuable to industry — silver, copper, lead and cadmium — the earth is a bonanza of gemstones and crystals, some of them on view in the local museum.

A final superlative: near the town of Grootfontein, the **Hoba Meteorite**, said to weigh 55 tons, is called the largest metal meteorite on earth. It was discovered here in the 1920s but it probably arrived from outer space thousands of years ago.

In the **Kunene** region (formerly Kaokoland), near Opuwo, the pastoral Himba people, numbering some 6,000, are descendants of Herero herders who fled to the

AfriPics.com/Max

A Himba girl with hair and skin covered in a red cosmetic.

northwest when they were displaced by the Nama. The women are noted for their intricate hairstyles and jewellery of shell, copper and iron. Both men and women anoint their bodies with a cream made from rancid butterfat, ochre powder and an aromatic resin. This gives the skin a reddish sheen which corresponds to the Himba ideal of beauty. They wear few clothes apart from a loin cloth or skirt of goat skin. The men handle politics and judicial problems, while the women do most of the manual labour.

Dining Out

This is carnivore country, where the inviting aroma of an outdoor barbecue often fills the air. The local beef is good, but you might want to try something more specifically Namibian—venison or warthog, for example, or even zebra.

On the coast the accent easily switches from steaks and chops to fresh fish or seafood (for instance Lüderitz oysters and Namibian rock lobsters).

Thanks to the German connection, the menu will also include tasty sausages, salamis and a variety of smoked meats to be consumed with copious amounts of pickled cabbage *(sauerkraut)*. They can be accompanied by an imaginative spectrum of breads and rolls, and followed by desserts (such as *Apfelstrudel* and *Schwarzwälder Kirschtorte*) so sumptuous they'll put your self-control at risk.

Drinks

Two influences—German taste and the climate—coincide here to make beer drinking a popular pastime. The local beer is brewed according to grand old traditions formalized in the 16th century, but because of the hot climate the alcohol content is usually kept a few degrees lower than the European equivalent.

South African wines, which include some first-class vintages, are also available. They have been making Cape wine since the 17th century. Most are identified by grower and grape variety: shiraz, cabernet sauvignon and the local hybrid pinotage among the reds; chardonnay, sauvignon blanc and chenin blanc the main whites.

Shopping

The map of Namibia shows a swathe of the southwest marked, intriguingly, "Diamond Area 1 (Restricted Area)". Some of the baubles lying about there turn up in the shops—diamonds and semi-precious stones like topaz and tourmaline. And consider the hand-made jewellery with traditional African motifs, usually of high quality.

Another Namibian speciality is fur. Karakul, a variety of Persian lamb, is fashioned into stylish garments under the Swakara name. Leather goods are interesting, though here the source may be buffalo or ostrich.

Among native curios, look for dolls in Herero costumes, hand-carved tribal trinkets, Himba beads and jewellery, pottery and basketwork.

On certain goods, such as jewellery, overseas visitors are exempt from the local sales tax.

PRACTICAL INFORMATION

Banks. Open Monday to Friday 9 a.m.–3.30 p.m., Saturdays until 11 a.m.

Clothing. In winter days are mild to warm, so you will need light summer clothes. But be prepared for chilly nights, even in summer.

Credit cards. Most shops, hotels, rest camps and restaurants accept internationally known credit cards, which can be used to draw money from ATMs in Windoek and other large towns, but not in more remote areas.

Currency. The Namibian dollar issued in notes of N$10 to N$200, and coins of 5 cents to N$5. It has the same value as the South African rand, which is accepted as legal tender.

Customs allowance. Travellers over 16 years of age may import duty-free 400 cigarettes and 50 cigars and 250 g of tobacco; 2 litres of wine and 1 litre of spirits; 50 ml of perfume and 250 ml of toilet water; other gift articles up to a value of N$50,000.

Driving. Namibia drives on the left. There is a general speed limit of 120 kph on open roads; reduce speed on gravel roads. Safety belts must be worn. Roads are clearly signposted. To hire a vehicle, you must be in possession of a valid international driver's licence. Cars and four-wheel-drive vehicles can be hired at Windhoek Airport and in Windhoek, Tsumeb, Walvis Bay and Swakopmund.

Electricity. 220/240 volts, 50 cycles AC. Plugs have three pins.

Health. Travellers to the northern parts of Namibia are advised to take anti-malaria precautions.

Language. English is the official language. German and Afrikaans are also widely spoken, and there are a dozen indigenous languages.

Telephone. To make an international call dial 001, then the country code (1 for Canada and US, 44 for UK), the area code and local number.

Tipping. It is usual to add a 10 per cent tip in restaurants.

Water. In the towns, the tap water is purified. In the countryside, some tap water, though fit for drinking, may taste salty.

Produced by seasonal flooding, the Okavango is the world's largest inland delta.

BOTSWANA

Luxury hotels and game lodges exist, but on the whole Botswana is a land of rugged, unspoiled wilderness. This is not a destination for the timid, what with the heat and the dust, and the chance of undisciplined elephants wandering into your path. The nearest filling station and water supply may be a long drive away.

But if you persevere, the sights are unique, uplifting, unforgettable. They include lonely landscapes as varied as deserts and lagoons, and dozens of species of wildlife from lions and leopards to giraffes and hippopotamuses. Hundreds of bird species are on show, and the reptiles range from dangerous snakes to dangerous crocodiles.

Botswana is very thinly populated, with about 1.9 million inhabitants, including nomadic San in the mysterious Kalahari desert, which spreads over more than half of the country. The majority, overwhelmingly rural, clusters near the borders of South Africa and Zimbabwe. Many other countries might well envy Botswana its democracy and strong economic growth. The republic's parliamentary system has worked well since independence was won in 1966. The wealth came shortly afterwards, with the discovery of enormous diamond reserves. Until then the economy had been based on cattle-rearing, and livestock is still another tidy export earner. Botswana is, however, a rather expensive country for travellers.

The towns, starting with the capital, Gaborone, have points of interest but they're mainly staging posts for the big attractions— the 17 per cent of the country dedicated to preserving wildlife and nature in general. Chobe National Park is the home of giant herds of elephant and buffalo, while Kgalagadi Transfrontier Park is the place to see lion and cheetah. The most unusual reserve is the Okavango Basin in the north, the earth's greatest inland river delta, surrounded by desert. The water attracts elephants, hippos, zebras and giraffes. You can explore it in a dugout canoe, but don't mistake a snoozing crocodile for a floating log.

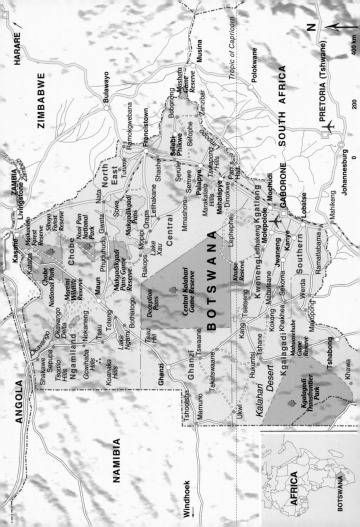

A BRIEF HISTORY

Early times
Ancestors of today's San ("Bushmen") and Khoe ("Hottentots") leave tools and wall paintings in Botswana, around 25,000 BC.

1st–8th centuries
Bantu migration arrives from central Africa. Farming andmining communities develop.

14th century
Tswana clans (Batswana) of the Bantu people settle in the land.

19th century
Expansionist Zulu warriors threaten stability, setting off migrations of terrorized tribes in southern Africa. In 1820 the London Missionary Society sends Robert Moffat to convert the Batswana to Christianity. Later the Society's David Livingstone establishes a mission. Gold is discovered near Francistown (1866). Alarmed at inroads of the Boers from South Africa, Khama asks for British protection. In 1885, to curb German influence in South West Africa and contain the Boers, Britain proclaims the protectorate of Bechuanaland. The capital is placed in Mafeking, South Africa. Britain proposes giving Bechuanaland administration to the British South Africa Company, run by tycoon Cecil Rhodes. Tribal chiefs go to London to plead for the status quo. Britain accedes but gives a strip of land to Rhodes for construction of his "Cape to Cairo" railway.

20th century–present
After Britain's victory in the Boer War, the Union of South Africa is established (1910). South Africa proposes to absorb Bechuanaland but tribal chiefs resist. The British create an African Advisory Council in 1920, giving the Batswana a voice in the protectorate's government. In 1948, studying law at Oxford, the Chief Seretse Khama marries a white Englishwoman, sparking a crisis in Bechuanaland. Seretse Khama becomes leader of the Bechuanaland Democratic Party (BDP), which wins the first free legislative elections. Britain grants independence in 1966, Sir Seretse Khama takes over the presidency of the new Republic of Botswana. Re-elected three times, Sir Seretse Khama dies in 1980. He is succeeded by Dr Quett Masire. In 2004 Festus Mogae is re-elected president; he is succeeded by Lt-Gen Ian Khama, the son of Seretse Khama, in 2008.

You'll have the chance to get close to the elephants in Botswana.

SIGHTSEEING

The wilderness is beyond compare in Botswana, and there's plenty of it, but you have to start somewhere. We begin in the national capital, the destination for some international flights (though many visitors route via Johannesburg direct to the "safari capital" Maun, bypassing Gaborone completely).

Gaborone

Until independence, administrative power was south of the border in Mafeking (now Mahikeng), South Africa. Since then the new capital of Botswana, Gaborone, has grown rapidly and now counts more than one in ten of the nation's inhabitants. Expansion has been so drastic that the city is often dismissed as being characterless—just a modern sprawl around the financial and administrative centre.

Until recently, Gaborone was mainly a transit point for the visitor rather than a sightseeing goal in itself. But ever since Mma Ramotswe, heroine of Alexander McCall Smith's Ladies Detective Agency novels, set up shop there, it has become the popular focus of local tours, taking in her house on Zebra Drive and her office at the garage, before setting off for Mochudi, Molepolole and other towns featuring in the novels.

While you're in Gaborone, getting accustomed to the climate, making plans, changing money and shopping along the nicely laid out Mall, take time out to visit the **National Museum and Art Gallery**. The museum provides a briefing on the Kalahari Desert, the lifestyle of its nomads, and the country's wildlife. The art is African and European, not just from Botswana.

Serowe

Between Gaborone and Francistown, Serowe is Botswana's largest village, with a population of 60,000. It is also the home of the Khama royal family. A statue honours the first president of Botswana, Sir Seretse Khama, and the **Khama III Memorial Museum** is devoted to the family's history in the 19th and 20th centuries. There are documents, uniforms and weapons. The museum, occupying the Red House, the

Kalahari glitter. Serowe shares in the prosperity of Botswana's diamond rush. Hundreds of villagers are employed to process and polish some of the gems unearthed in the Kalahari. The first Botswana diamond field, discovered in 1967, was at Orapa, northwest of Serowe. But the biggest diamond mine was found in 1973 at Jwaneng, west of Gaborone. Security at the diamond sites is extremely vigilant; guided tours are not yet on the menu.

family home, also has exhibits on the life of the local Bangwato people and the Bushmen. A room is devoted to Botswana's best-loved writer Bessie Head (1937–86), author of *Serowe: Village of the Rain Wind*. There is also a natural history display, which includes snakes and more than a thousand species of insect.

Francistown

Linked to Gaborone by air, rail and a good road, Botswana's oldest city, Francistown, has been around since the gold rush of the 1860s. Most of the gold ran out, but not the less glamorous minerals, and the town was also able to keep going with agriculture and industry. Some atmospheric 19th-century buildings, like the old railway station, the jail and the courthouse, have been preserved. In the metropolis of the northeast you'll also find good hotels and shopping facilities, as well as a cinema.

Maun

Many safaris start in Maun, a Wild West sort of town on the edge of the wondrous Okavango Delta. Its name means Place of the Black Reeds. The principal school of architecture here is the mud hut, to which some imaginative inhabitants have added extra interest by incorporating old soft-drink cans into the walls. Cattle wander freely along the dusty streets. So does a cast of characters ranging from authentic African villagers to expat tour guides, naturalists and hunters just back from the bush. Maun is the town for organizing a safari, or stocking up on provisions before setting forth, or sampling a few comforts of civilization after a tough time in the wilds.

National Parks

The animals and the birds, the scenery and the solitude are wonderfully preserved in Botswana's national parks and reserves. Accommodation ranges from the most lavish of lodges with en-suite bathrooms to spartan camp sites with the barest of necessities. But the nation's tourist pol-

icy aims to discourage crowds of backpackers in favour of a fairly limited number of big spenders, so you may have little choice but to wallow in luxury between excursions.

Gaborone Game Reserve

For tourists swooping in and out, the Gaborone Game Reserve, on the edge of the capital, gives a useful preview of some of the wildlife on show at the major national parks. Established in 1988 and only 600 ha in extent, it is nevertheless the third busiest wildlife destination in the country, as urban commuters and tourists in transit can head out for a quick morning excursion to see wildebeest, zebra, white rhino and several kinds of antelope. Early mornings and evenings are the best times for game spotting, but the reserve closes at 6.30 p.m.

istockphoto.com/Malsbury

Okavango Delta

Rivers always flow towards the sea, or try to, but the Okavango, which originates in Angola, is thwarted by geological fate. Unable to reach the Indian Ocean because of changes in the earth's crust, it spills into the sands of the

flickr.com/Huber

A water-lily lagoon in the Okavango delta, also home to the Malachite kingfisher (Alcedo cristata) and the painted reed frog (Hyperolius marmoratus).

Dugout in the delta. The local equivalent of a Venetian gondolier is the poler who propels his dugout canoe through the labyrinth of the Okavango Delta. Maps are of little use in a constantly shifting pattern of waterways, so the poler has to know where he's going—and many channels are barely deep enough for the shallow-draught boat to get through. The *mokoro*, fashioned from a single log, can accommodate three passengers. The best polers add a lot to the experience by pointing out and identifying the birds and animals along the way.

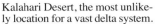

istockphoto.com//Karock

Kalahari Desert, the most unlikely location for a vast delta system.

At the flood, the water swells to cover an area of more than 16,000 sq km (6,000 sq miles), much of it forming lagoons dotted with water lilies and shallow, narrow channels that are invaded by papyrus reeds.

All this clear, cool water attracts a wide variety of mammals along with 450 bird and 80 fish species, but the antelope, zebras and baboons are almost secondary to the sheer wonder of the setting, the atmosphere of nature at its unspoiled best. Small aircraft fly from Maun to safari camps on islands in the delta—the flight alone is a thrilling introduction to the beauty and mystery of it all. The way to explore the delta at a leisurely pace is aboard a *mokoro* (plural *mekoro*), a flat-bottomed dugout canoe poled through the lilies and reeds by a knowledgeable navigator.

Moremi Wildlife Reserve

On the northeast of the Okavango Delta, the Moremi Wildlife Reserve packs a full range of landscapes into 1,800 sq km (700 sq miles)—acacia forests, floodlands, lagoons and reedy swamps. Thanks to the remarkable diversity of wilderness, the reserve can be seen by land or water or both. As varied as the terrain is the game, from lion and leopard to elephant and buffalo. And the birds—storks, herons, eagles and bee-eaters—lift the eyes and the hearts of even the least informed.

In 1963, local Tswana tribes donated this land to the nation to make sure the region's wildlife and ecosystem would never be disturbed.

Tsodilo Hills

Northwest of the delta, near Namibia's Caprivi Strip, four big rocky hills rise above the dunes. Thanks to the mystique of the hills and the availability of spring water, the area has been inhabited for thousands of years, as witness a profusion of rock paintings— more than 4500 images of animals (some of them now extinct), of abstractions and geometric doodles and, less frequently, of humans. They are thought to have been painted by the distant ancestors of the Basarwa and Bantu peoples who still inhabit the area. It is a UNESCO World Heritage site.

Four quartzite hills stand in a row. Three of them were given names by the Bushmen: Male, Female and Child, while the smallest hill remains nameless. Most of the art work, Botswana's greatest archaeological treasure, is concentrated about the Female hill. The explorer and author Laurens van der Post called this "a Louvre of the desert".

flickr.com/Huber

The rhinoceros are among the most famous paintings in the Tsodilo Hills.

Chobe National Park

The best time to visit Chobe, in northeastern Botswana, is from May to September, when a single day's tour can reveal thousands of animals—elephants in unparalleled numbers (too many for the good of the environment), buffalo, hippo, giraffe, kudu and impala. More than 250 species of birds are also viewable. The area of the park, more than 11,000 sq km (4,500 sq miles) is about the size of Jamaica or the state of Connecticut. The accommodation ranges from crowded campsites to the sumptuous game lodge where Richard Burton and Elizabeth Taylor spent their second honeymoon in the requisite degree of luxury.

Serondella, the northern district of the park, borders the Chobe River, which has its source in Angola. It provides drinking and bathing facilities for throngs of elephants and buffalo. The landscape here is an incomparable combination of flood plains and riverine woodland. Set out along the river bank, the town that services this part of the park, **Kasane**, is equipped with everything from car hire firms and safari organizers to a bank and post office.

The central area, **Ngwezumba**, is rich in animal life, especially when the rains have refilled the pans in, say, November to May.

Savuti is the southwestern portion of the park, and rich in fauna from November to May. The Mababe Depression is the bed of an ancient lake that once covered most of northern Botswana. It is now a flat plain that comes to life when it rains. A sand ridge more than 100 km (60 miles) long shows one boundary of the great lake, which has long since dried up. Even when water is relatively scarce the animals enjoy munching the greenery.

Nxai Pan National Park

During the rainy season, from November to March, the ancient lake bed turns green. Then graceful zebras, gemsboks and springboks and clumsy wildebeest flock to the Nxai Pan to nibble the grass, drink and breed. The area is also renowned for its population of giraffes and leopards. Migratory birds make this a seasonal halt, to the delight of binocular-wielding bird-watchers. A landmark south of the reserve is a grove of baobab trees, named

---

Botswana's Big Five. There are so many elephants in Botswana's national parks, and they are such immense targets, that you can hardly miss seeing or photographing a herd. However, the other species of "the big five" may prove more elusive. Cape buffalo, with their great curving horns, are endangered by trophy hunters and local meat-eaters, but they should be easily visible. The leopard keeps to itself, sleeping most of the day up in a tree and hunting by night. Lions are gregarious but hard to spot in the bush; best seen around water sources in the dry season. Finally, the rhinoceros, a vegetarian, has been hunted mercilessly and makes few appearances except early morning and late afternoon at water holes. Nevertheless, picturesque animals such as zebra, giraffe and antelope are abundant.

Baines' Baobabs after Thomas Baines, the artist who painted them in 1862. Thick-trunked baobabs, known in some circles as monkey-bread trees, produce fruit which has medicinal uses. The branches also provide welcome shade, and this particular crop, forming "one magnificent shade", as Baines wrote, is really memorable.

Makgadikgadi Pans

Once upon a time there was a lake bigger than Lake Victoria here, but it all dried up—a very distant memory that's revived in the rainy season. All that's left of the prehistoric lake are large depressions called salt pans, just the sort of environment to attract waterfowl. This is the place to admire a huge blush of pink flamingos. The plains to the west, which are not saturated with salt like the remains of the lake, abound in wildlife, especially after the rains arrive in October or November. The area is a main migration route for antelope and the predators that follow them.

For tourists, four-wheel drive is the only feasible means of locomotion for Nxai Pan and Makgadikgadi reserves.

Central Kalahari Game Reserve

In the very centre of Botswana, the world's second largest game reserve is bigger than some

flickr.com/Gray

You will no doubt meet San people in the Kalahari desert.

respectably sized European countries—for instance Denmark, Switzerland or the Netherlands. This is essentially virgin territory—no roads, no campsites—and the government has wanted to keep it that way. You need a special permit to visit the reserve.

One of the few landmarks has the strikingly evocative name of Deception Valley. Depending on the rainfall the animals may be thinner on the ground than you'd expect to find in reserves with reliable water sources. But the antelope know how to survive

DRIVING IN THE BUSH

If you're on a drive-yourself safari through Botswana's bush or desert or swamplands, you're in for a rugged experience.

The first essential is knowing your vehicle. Get used to the four-wheel-drive capability before you ever leave the comfort of the surfaced roads; have a test drive when you first encounter difficult conditions. Driving in endless tracts of sand or mud will test all your talents—and those of the vehicle.

Be on the lookout for wild animals—not just for the thrill of seeing and photographing them but to keep clear of them. Yield the right of way to any sort of livestock, from a lost goat to a troop of elephants. If animals are near, don't get out of your car or even put your arms out the windows. There are no animals, however appealing, that don't pose a danger. Don't feed any wild animal.

Driving at night, even on tarred roads, is extremely hazardous. Anything may suddenly cross your path, from ranch cattle to wild animals. The danger is heightened in winter when the paving, which retains some of the day's heat, attracts the wildlife. Use bright headlights and spotlight if available. Even better, don't drive at all once the sun has gone down.

Although the main highways are surfaced, much of Botswana's road network consists of gravel or sand tracks. This means that oncoming traffic kicks up a great storm, cutting visibility and posing many dangers ahead. When you see someone approaching, drive very slowly or pull over and switch on your lights.

istockphoto.com/Fogel

drought on the moisture in the vegetation. Meanwhile, the grandeur and silence of the Kalahari Desert are all around.

Khutse Game Reserve

About 240 km (150 miles) northwest of Gaborone, Khutse is the closest nature reserve to the capital, though four-wheel drive is required to get there. Elementary campsites for travellers self-sufficient in everything from water to fuel and food are the only luxury in this small reserve adjoining the Central Kalahari Game Reserve to the north.

You may encounter Bushmen who can provide knowledgeable insight into desert life and wildlife and the way to survive the Kalahari's rigours. After the rains have fallen this reserve is a gathering place for lions, leopards and their prey, and a fine range of birds.

Kgalagadi Transfrontier Park

Wildlife without frontiers: the antelope have never needed passports or visas to migrate from the Botswana portion of the national park to the South African section; in fact, there are no fences. Until 2000 the Gemsbok National Park in Botswana and the Kalahari Gemsbok National Park in South Africa were managed separately, but they have now merged and were renamed.

In the desert the game may have to travel great distances to find the water and food they require. But two usually dry rivers, the Auob and the Nossob, cut through the dunes, and when it rains they flourish. Among the animals you may see are gemsbok, wildebeest, eland and springbok—all closely followed by the lions and cheetahs who live in hope of ambushing them, and nature's competent clean-up squad of hyenas and jackals. More than 200 species of bird brighten the park. One extraordinary species, the sociable weaver bird (Philetiarus socius), builds gigantic nests in trees, subdivided into "apartments" for as many as 100 couples.

Mabuasehube Game Reserve

This small game reserve, on the eastern edge of the Kgalagadi Transfrontier Park, is difficult to reach, hence little visited. The name means "red soil", a curt description of the rust-hued Kalahari sands, which are permeated by iron oxide. The salt pans in the Mabuasehube are a big attraction in themselves, reflecting different colours according to the time of day. During the rainy season the pans, bordered by high dunes, call together thirsty gemsbok, springbok, eland and wildebeest, followed by lions and leopards, and birds galore.

Dining Out

With two head of cattle for every inhabitant, Botswana produces a mountain of beef. It's highly regarded for taste, and turns up on just about every restaurant menu, in the shape of steaks or burgers or meat pies. For a change, look for fried chicken or pizza. You may also be offered some of Botswana's fine river fish—bream. If you're craving fresh vegetables—and you probably will after a few days of corned beef in the bush—hasten to the buffet at one of the main hotels, where salads get pride of place.

The cuisine in general is reminiscent of British colonial days, but there are inspired exceptions at some of the luxury game lodges, where skilled cooks transform the best local and imported produce into inventive meals for sophisticated clients.

The diet of the average villager, by contrast, could hardly be less sophisticated. The staple is a tasteless but filling cornmeal mush called *mielie-pap*. Rounding out the menu are pumpkins, melons, cucumbers, beans and—for a special treat—grilled insects.

If you're in the bush you'll appreciate *biltong*, wind-dried strips of meat that need no refrigeration. Of beef or game, it can be as tasty as it is chewy.

Shopping

The range of souvenirs for sale in the craft outlets is dominated by basketwork. Look for baskets, trays and toys, some of a very high standard, woven from palm leaves. Agile craftsmen also produce wood carvings, mainly inspired by the local fauna, pottery and jewellery. Weavers offer wall-hangings, tablecloths and clothing. The Bushmen create beaded bracelets and belts, using chips of ostrich egg shells as beads. Another unique souvenir is a Bushman bow-and-arrow hunting set.

You may be tempted by animal skins, which are acquired from culling drives. Another aspect of the skin trade: products of crocodile skin, such as wallets and briefcases. But before buying anything like this, check your country's import regulations!

istockphoto.com/Lamb

PRACTICAL INFORMATION

Banks. Open Monday–Friday 9 a.m.–2.30 p.m. and Saturdays 8.15–10.45 a.m.

Climate. The seasons south of the equator are reversed. Summer, which lasts from October to April, is also the rainy season. May to September is cooler and drier. Early morning temperatures may approach the freezing point in winter.

Credit cards of most of the international brands are accepted on a limited basis. Travellers cheques may be exchanged at banks and hotels.

Currency. The currency is the *pula* (P), divided into 100 *thebe*. Banknotes come in denominations from P10 to P100, coins from 5 thebe to P5.

Customs allowance. Visitors may import duty-free 400 cigarettes and 50 cigars and 250 g tobacco; 2 litres of wine and 1 litre of alcoholic beverages; 250 ml of toilet water and 50 ml of perfume; other gift articles up to a value of P500. No restrictions on the import of foreign currency (which must be declared on arrival), but no more than P50 in local currency may be exported.

Driving. Roads link the main towns. Drive on the left. The speed limit on country roads is 120 km per hour (75 mph).

Electricity. 220/240 volts, 50 cycles AC.

Health. Visitors to the northern parts of the country from November to June are advised to take anti-malaria precautions.

Languages. The official languages are Setswana and English.

Photography. Ask permission before you snap local people. Don't film defence establishments, airports or official government residences.

Shops are generally open Monday to Friday 8.30 a.m.–1 p.m. and 2–5 p.m. and again on Saturday mornings.

Taxis. Fares should be agreed on before starting out.

Time. UTC/GMT + 2 all year round.

Telephone. To make an international call, dial 00 then the country code (1 for Canada and US, 44 for UK), the area code and local number. There are very few public phone boxes.

Tipping. The standard tip in urban areas is 10 per cent.

Water. Drinking water is considered safe in towns and hotels. Don't drink from (or swim in!) rivers.

The thundering waters of Victoria Falls, named by David Livingstone.

ZAMBIA

Shaped by three great rivers, the Republic of Zambia lies on a high plateau of Central Africa, with chains of hills rising up to 2,100 m (6,900 ft). So although it lies within the tropics, its elevation tempers the high temperatures and humidity usually associated with tropical countries.

Some 12 million people, including more than 70 Bantu-speaking tribes, live within its 752,620 sq km (290,590 sq miles) — considerably larger than Germany and Poland put together. The land-locked republic shares frontiers with, going clockwise from the north, the Democratic Republic of the Congo (formerly Zaire), Tanzania, Malawi, Mozambique, Zimbabwe, Botswana, Namibia and Angola. Besides the sprawling metropolis of the capital, Lusaka, the principal towns are Kitwe, Ndola, Kabwe and Livingstone. As this last suggests, Scottish explorer David Livingstone travelled through the areas around the Zambezi River and arrived at the stupendous cataract of "the smoke that thunders" on November 17, 1855. Patriotically, he named the Falls after Queen Victoria. It was on his second venture into Central Africa that he died of malaria in May 1873 at Chitambo, 100 km (62 miles) north of Serenje at the narrow "waist" of the country. The Livingstone Memorial marks the spot where his heart was buried; his body was carried by two faithful followers, Chuma and Sussi, to London and buried in Westminster Abbey in 1874.

Thanks to its wide range of habitats, there is a huge variety of flora and fauna, including big game, grazing animals, riverine species and a wealth of birdlife. Apart from safaris, the sporting activities range from abseiling and bungy jumping to river rafting and tiger-fishing.

For anyone in search of close encounters with nature, willing to rough it quite a lot in order to see wild animals that have not grown bored by the ever-intrusive cameras of massed safari tourists, Zambia offers new sensations and a worthy challenge. Not to mention the glorious sunsets.

A BRIEF HISTORY

Early times
The region is inhabited by San (Bushmen), who are later displaced by the Bantu tribes.

19th century
British Empire builder Cecil Rhodes obtains mining concessions in 1889 from King Lewanika of the Barotse, and settlers descend on the area.

20th century– present
As Northern Rhodesia, the country is administered by the British South Africa Company, established by Rhodes, until 1924 when the British government takes over the administration. From 1953 to 1963, it is linked with Southern Rhodesia and Nyasaland (now Zimbabwe and Malawi) in the Central African Federation. When the Federation is dissolved on December 31, 1963, Northern Rhodesia achieves internal self-government under a new constitution, and on October 24, 1964 it is named Zambia, an independent republic within the Commonwealth. Its first President is Dr Kenneth Kaunda, who lends moral support to neighbouring Southern Rhodesia in its struggle against white-dominated rule but manages to avoid that neighbour's protracted bout of guerrilla warfare. After a visit by President Kaunda to China in 1967, China finances a 1,600-km (1,000-mile) railroad from the Copperbelt to Dar es Salaam in Tanzania, thus giving Zambia vital access to the Indian Ocean and world markets. The country's economy remains highly susceptible to fluctuations in the global price of copper. In 1968 Zambia's oil supplies are also assured by the opening of a pipeline from Ndola in the Copperbelt to Dar es Salaam.

In July 1973, a new constitution is introduced, making the United National Independence Party (UNIP), headed by Kaunda, the only party. He remains president until being defeated in elections held in October 1991 which result in an end to one-party rule. Zambia's new government under President Frederick Chiluba, a former bus conductor, calls for sweeping economic reforms including privatization and the setting up of a stock market. Tourism begins to be more positively encouraged. Chiluba's Movement for Multiparty Democracy (MMD) wins a big majority in the 1996 presidential elections. Chiluba stands down in 2001 after failing in a bid to change the constitution to permit him to stand for a third term. Levy Mwanawasa of the MMD wins the elections and is re-elected in 2006; one of his priorities is tackling corruption. After his death in 2008 following a stroke, the vice president Rupiah Banda becomes president.

SIGHTSEEING

Zambia shares the Victoria Falls with Zimbabwe, and many visitors are day trippers coming over from the Zimbabwe side of the falls. But there is much else to see around the country, including spectacular sections of the other main rivers, the Kafue and the Luangwa, as well as the great swamplands in the region of Lake Bangweulu in the north and in the heartland of the country northwest of Lusaka. The frontiers also touch on three major lakes, Mweru, Tanganyika and man-made Kariba.

Lusaka

The capital, founded in 1905 and granted city status in 1960, now supports a population of more than 3 million. It is worth exploring for its lively street markets, shopping centres, restaurants and galleries of local artefacts. The strong contrast between smart modern city blocks on wide boulevards lined with flowering trees and shabby shacks makes for striking photographs.

Much of the action takes place in the **Cairo Road** area close to the railway and bus stations. A little beyond Cairo Road is **New City Market**, a bustling maze of stalls and vendors, and there are several other popular markets here and there. Take care not to carry visible goods of value or fat wallets to tempt pickpockets.

Other places to visit include the **Kabwata Cultural Centre**, the **Zintu Community Museum** of arts and crafts, and, further out of town, the **Munda Wanga Environmental Park** with zoo and botanical gardens and the **Kalimba Reptile Park** with family entertainment.

The **Namwandwe Art Gallery** lies some 15 km (10 miles) from the city centre, but other galleries in town offer paintings and carvings of high quality.

Victoria Falls

About twice as wide and twice as deep as Niagara, the Victoria Falls carry the mighty Zambezi River—545 million litres of water per minute—over a sheer precipice with a maximum drop of 108 m (355 ft), into a chasm

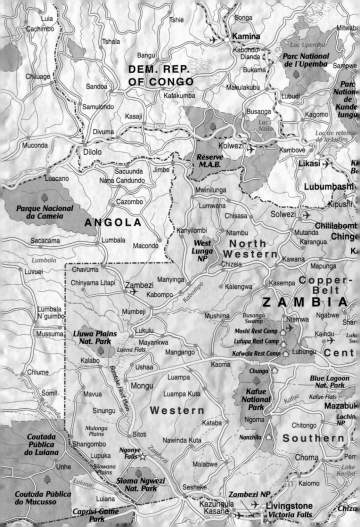

Luia
Cachimbo
Tshie
Songa
Mitwaba
Kamina
Kabondo-
Dianda
Parc National
de l'Upemba
Sampwe
Tshala
Bangu
Bukama
Parc
Nation
de
Kunde
Iungu
DEM. REP.
OF CONGO
Makulakubu
Chiluage
Sandoa
Katakumba
Lubudi
Kagomo
Lac de retenue
de la Lufira
Samulondo
Kasaji
Busanga
Lac
Nzilo
Divuma
Kolwezi
Kambove
Likasi
Muconda
Dilolo
Réserve
M.A.B.
Lubumbashi
Pushi
Luacano
Sacuunda
Nana Candundo
Jimbe
Mwinilunga
Chililabomt
Solwezi
Ching
Cazombo
Lumwana
Chisasa
Mutanda
Karangua
Parque Nacional
da Cameia
ANGOLA
Kanyilombi
Ntambu
North
Western
Kawana
Mapunga
Sacacama
Lumbala
Macondo
West
Lunga
NP
Chizela
Copper-
Belt
Lumbala
Chavuma
Manyinga
Kalengwa
Kasempa
ZAMBIA
Luvuei
Chinyama Litapi
Zambezi
Kabompo
Ngabwe
Shar
Lumbala
N'guimbo
Mumbeji
Mushima
Busanga
Swamp
Ntemwa
Moshi Rest Camp
Kaindu
Luke
Sw
Mussuma
Liuwa Plains
Nat. Park
Lukulu
Mayankwa
Lufupa Rest Camp
Lubungu
Cent
Liena Flats
Kafwala Rest Camp
Chiume
Kalabo
Mangango
Kaoma
M9
Chunga
Somil
Mavua
Ushaa
Luampa
Blue Lagoon
Nat. Park
Mongu
Luampa Kuta
Kafue
National
Park
Kafue Flats
Mazabuk
Sinungu
Western
Kataba
Ngoma
Chitongo
Lochin
NP
Mulonga
Plains
Sitoti
Nanzhila
Southern
Coutada
Pública
do Luiana
Shangombo
Lupuka
Nawinda Kuta
Malabwe
Choma
Pem
Ngonye
Falls
Unhe
Silowana
Plains
Zambezi
Lake
Kariba
Coutada Pública
do Mucusso
Luiana
Sioma Ngwezi
Nat. Park
Seshéke
Zambezi NP
Kalomo
Luiana
Kazungula
Kasane
Livingstone
Caprivi Game
Park
Chiza
Victoria Falls

Pens and crayons make excellent gifts for the children.

whose width varies from 25 to 75 m (80 to 240 ft). The Zambezi thunders down into the gorge leading to the Boiling Pot. Just below this maelstrom of dashing water, the gorge is spanned by the Victoria Falls Bridge, 111 m (364 ft) high, carrying rail, road and pedestrian traffic between Zambia and Zimbabwe. The **Victoria Falls National Park** lies in Zimbabwe, and it is from that side that the most familiar views are taken. The Zimbabwe side has a busier airport than the small Livingstone International Airport, and more tourist facilities. The small town here, within walking distance of the falls, has good hotels, shops, even a casino, and agencies that organize all sorts of outings. In the centre of town, the **Falls Craft Village** is laid out like a tribal settlement, but the huts have been transplanted from various regions.

On the other hand, the Zambian side gives you closest access to Mosi-oa-Tunya, or the Smoke that Thunders, as the early inhabitants of the area called the falls. The mist and spray may reach 500 m (1,640 ft) into the sky and can be seen 30 km (18 miles) away. Walkways lead down to the foot of the falls at the **Boiling Pot**, while the main trail heads through the dense clouds of spray and across a hairy footbridge to **Knife Edge Point** poised above the abyss. This offers the finest view of the Eastern Cataract and the main falls. You can also watch intrepid thrill-seekers bungyjumping from the Victoria Falls Bridge. White-water rafting is also available in the gorge, and microlight and helicopter flights over the falls and gorge can be arranged. Periods of full moon offer the unique spectacle of a nighttime rainbow amid the spray. In the dry season, it is sometimes possible to walk across the riverbed to Livingstone Island.

You can drive around the small **Mosi-o-Tunya National Park** in the space of a few hours. It is home to giraffe, zebra and half a dozen white rhino, among the last survivors of this endangered species.

Livingstone, a small but booming town a short distance north of the Falls, has several arts and crafts markets. The Livingstone Museum is Zambia's national museum, ranging over the country's long history and displaying archaeological artefacts as well as letters and other memorabilia of Livingstone himself.

The **Kariba Dam**, built in the 1950s, created Lake Kariba, one of the biggest man-made lakes in the world, 280 km (175 miles) in length. It supplies both Zambia and Zimbabwe with hydroelectric power. The Zambian shore is less developed for tourism than the Zimbabwean side, but efforts are being made to improve boating and fishing facilities.

National Parks

Most of the national parks are administered by the Zambia Wildlife Authority. First time visitors not booked onto an organized safari might think about hiring a game scout or guide at any park they visit.

Relatively near to Lusaka, **Lower Zambezi National Park** is an attractive game reserve covering about 4,000 sq km (1,544 sq miles) on the northern bank of the river. There are several camps in the park and a network of internal roads offers good game viewing, with lion and elephant both prolific, and leopard often to be encountered on night drives. Fishing excursions are available, but the speciality here is thrilling day or overnight canoeing trips

Park life. Zambia has 19 national parks and 36 game management areas (GMAs), all of them with a wealth of mammal and bird life. Entrance fees vary considerably, but several make no charge. Accommodation ranges from luxury hotels, through more simple safari lodges providing meals and other services, down to little more than basic huts to which visitors must bring their own food, cooking gear and fuel. No hunting is allowed in the national parks, but is permitted, under tight control, in the GMAs. Away from the main towns, roads are poorly maintained and at frequent risk from flooding. Car hire is possible in the main towns, but four-wheel drive vehicles are well-nigh essential for cross-country expeditions. Most travel agencies would recommend joining organized safari tours with reliable vehicles and sound security arrangements. The Zambian government is committed to building up the tourism industry, in partnership with the private sector.

along a stretch of the Zambezi teeming with hippos, crocs, water birds and terrestrial wildlife.

South Luangwa National Park rates among the best game parks in all of Africa. It lies on the Luangwa River in Eastern Zambia and covers some 9,050 sq km (3,490 sq miles) of plains, woodland and grassland. When the river floods between December and March, the area is transformed into a rich, highly productive ecosystem of dramatic scenic beauty. Beside the "big game," impala, puku and zebra can be seen here in abundance, as well as Thornicroft's giraffe, differing in coloration from the more common species found elsewhere in Africa. Leopard "hunts" by night are something of a speciality. Sixty different species of mammal have been counted here, and some 400 species of bird. Birdlife is particularly intense in the Nsefu Sector, where the Luangwa serpents its way through and between a series of lagoons. The best period for viewing is during or just after the rainy season. Most of lodges and camps, open year-round, are run by safari companies, whose representatives meet visitors at Lusaka Airport and fly them to nearby Mfuwe airfield. Night drives, safaris on horseback and river rides as well as trips in open-top vehicles are all available; the network of game-viewing roads is recommended for only 4 x 4 vehicles. Walking safaris are a special feature here; the legendary Zambian game warden Norman Carr is credited with pioneering the walking safari as opposed to the shooting safari in the Luangwa Valley back in the 1960s. He was the first to promote the idea that income from wildlife tourism should support local communities.

Wildlife in profusion. Because of the diverse ecology of the country, the list of animal life in Zambia is so long that only the flavour of it can be given here. It ranges from elephant, rhino, hippo, lion, leopard, cheetah, jackal and hyena, through crocodile, various snakes (including puff adders and spitting cobras), aardvark, buffalo, giraffe, wildebeest and zebra, to baboon, bush baby, mongoose, monkey, warthog and a great many species of antelope. Insects, too, are plentiful! The spectrum of birdlife, since it spans raptors, river birds, swamp dwellers and those species that prefer grassland or high plateaus, rain forests or dry miombo woodlands, is no less varied. In fact, no fewer than 740 species have been recorded, including the endemic Chaplin's barbet. A comprehensive list can be found on the Zambia Tourist Board's excellent website at: www.zambiatourism.com

Only half the size of its neighbour, **North Luangwa National Park** is less accessible and therefore less visited, but shares much of the same flora and fauna as its big sister. There are estimated to be at least 50 hippos per kilometre of the Luangwa River. Safaris on foot are organized as the terrain is generally too rough even for off-road vehicles. Private groups are not permitted in the park and only two safari operators are authorized to arrange tours.

Lying between the two last-mentioned areas, the small **Luambe National Park** spans about 240 sq km (90 sq miles) of flood plains of the Luangwa River in the east of the country. Visitors must carry all the supplies and equipment they will need, and the single road is impassable in the wet season. Here as elsewhere, precautions should be taken against mosquitoes and tsetse flies.

Worth a detour off the Mpika to Isoka road in northeastern Zambia is **Shiwa Ng'andu**, a manor house built in Tuscan style by an English eccentric, Sir Stewart Gore-Browne, who died in 1967 and was buried on the estate with all the honours of an African chief. With a tall clocktower and set amid recognizably English gardens, the house is a kind of decaying shrine to benign colonialism.

flickr.com/molcho

Thornicroft's giraffe can be seen in South Luangwa National Park. Its hairy knobs are called ossicones.

Further to the west is the **Lavushi Manda National Park**, covering 1,500 sq km (580 sq miles) of woodlands on the slopes of Lavushi Mountain. Poaching has wrought havoc with big game, but it is bracing walking country for the adventurous-minded. Visitors have to be self-sufficient as there are no tourist facilities in the reserve; understandably, they are advised to beware of dangerous animals when camping.

The small **Kasanka National Park** lies to the south of the extensive

Safety. Lusaka has an unhappy reputation for theft and mugging. Be streetwise; take advice from your hotel or lodgings about which areas of the city to avoid. Always keep as if you know where you are going. Don't carry more cash than you need for daily use, don't flaunt high-tech gadgetry about your person, try to blend in with the locals to the degree possible and don't risk lone walks by night. It is best always to leave someone to guard your car when you park, as thefts from cars and of cars are frequent. That said, the majority of Zambians are well-disposed towards foreign visitors and very ready to offer help and advice.

Lake Bangweulu swamps. It is privately run by the Kasanka Trust, which ploughs back all receipts from tourism into conserving the wild life and helping local communities. Birdlife is prolific and, since the swamplands are interspersed with wide grasslands, there are many antelope species, including the localized black lechwe.

The **Sumbu (Nsumbu) National Park** in Northern Zambia spans over 2,000 sq km (770 sq miles) of miombo woodland and open grassland, and is bounded to the north by Lake Tanganyika, which is the world's longest, second-deepest, and second-most voluminous freshwater body. The authorities are trying to build up this little-visited area into a more attractive and thriving tourist attraction, and the park itself holds a wealth of animal and bird species. The park is regarded as good lion country. People do swim and even scuba-dive in the lake but, quite apart from hippos and crocodiles, there may be a risk of bilharzia, the parasite that causes schistosomiasis. In the southeast corner of the lake lies **Mpulungu**, a bustling port whose lake traffic gives Zambia access to the heartland of Central Africa. On the border with Tanzania, the Kalambo Falls, at 221 m (725 ft) are Africa's second-highest.

Lochinvar National Park lies amid flood plains on the southern bank of the Kafue River some 80 km (50 miles) southwest of Lusaka. Though small, it is an outstanding bird sanctuary, with more than 400 species of birds recorded, and has been designated "a wetland of international importance" by the World Wide Fund for Nature. Besides the birds, there are wildebeest, kudu, oribi, zebra and hippo to be seen. Accommodation is limited and visitors must carry with them all the food and petrol they will need. The same is true of the **Blue Lagoon National Park**, further to the north, which is even more difficult of access and is best seen in the rainy season when the birdlife is spectacular.

Kafue National Park lying about 200 km (120 miles) to the west of Lusaka is Zambia's largest, at 22,400 sq km (8,648 sq miles)—larger than Wales or the State of Massachusetts. The Kafue River and its tributaries the Lufupa and the Lunga cause seasonal flooding and swamplands, which attract abundant birdlife, while the grasslands are home to plentiful big game. Accommodation at several of the lodges is in thatched huts, and the park's camps are open all year round, offering game-viewing drives, fishing and bird-watching boat trips. Four-wheel drive vehicles are essential for the rough park tracks. Visitors are advised to take special precautions against malaria.

About 300 km (185 miles) upstream from the Victoria Falls, the Zambezi plunges in a great tumult of cascades through a long narrow gorge, explored by Livingstone in 1853. These are the **Ngonye Falls**, also known as the Sioma Falls, very spectacular in themselves and without the hurly-burly of mass tourism. Nearby is the little-visited **Sioma Ngwezi National Park** and the more distant **Liuwa Plains National Park**. The former consists of dense woodland, with an appropriate richness of grazing animals and their predators; the Kwando River forms the southwestern border, and is also the frontier with Angola. Liuwa Plains is largely grassland so animal and bird life is abundant, but poachers pose a potential threat and visitors are advised to go with an official armed game scout.

Dining Out

Fast food eateries with fixed fare and takeaway meals are proliferating, especially in Lusaka and Livingstone and near the Victoria Falls. Take local advice to find restaurants and cafés where tourists will not feel out of place and the food is reliable. Hotel restaurants serve international food as well as Zambian specialities. Up-country, of course, the range is limited, and visitors must be prepared to rough it. Some filling-stations have small cafés attached, but most of the time you will have to take pot luck. Anyone intending touring for several days will carry provisions and the means to cook them; self-catering facilities are routinely available on safari.

Vegetarians are out of luck; meals here are based on meat—tender, juicy, fat steaks, usually barbecued (*braai*). Fresh lake fish is also available. There are plenty of potatoes but vegetables are limited, on the whole, to cabbage and onions. Tomatoes, mangoes and bananas add some colour and variety.

The villagers' staple diet is corn mush (*nshima*) accompanied by meat, fish or vegetables, and gravy.

Drinks

The favourite drink is beer, which is brewed in Zambia, the most popular brands being Mosi, Castle and Rhino. South African wines are available in hotels and lodges.

Shopping

The bright colours and traditional patterns of African cloth, wood-carvings, beadwork, metal jewellery and pottery make attractive presents to carry home. Beautiful baskets are made from bamboo, bark, grasses, papyrus, rushes or sisal. Shop around and make comparisons before taking the plunge, and even then don't be afraid to bargain—but always with good humour.

Zambia is an important source of gemstones such as emeralds, amethysts and garnets. They can be exported, usually uncut, but it is illegal to buy from unregistered sources, and the law will not protect you if you are cheated. Local purchases of cut gemstones and jewellery incur a 17.5 per cent value-added tax.

CDs of African music are readily available, as are drums and other musical instruments.

Health precautions. Although there is no insistence on vaccinations before entering Zambia, travellers should have up-to-date tetanus, diphtheria and polio vaccinations. Vaccination against hepatitis A and B and typhoid is also advised by the WHO. Mosquitoes may carry malaria, so cover up against them, especially in the evening, and sleep under insecticide-treated bed nets. Start anti-malarial drugs a full week before leaving home, follow the regular dosage to the letter, and continue taking the drugs for four weeks after leaving Africa. On safari, cover up too against tsetse flies. Western Zambia, adjoining Angola, is endemic for yellow fever, so vaccination against this mosquito-borne disease is advised (though it is not obligatory) for travellers intending to make a long stay there. AIDS is a serious problem in Zambia.

Stomach upsets are well-nigh unavoidable, but most resolve themselves without need of medication. Seasoned travellers always carry anti-diarrhoea pills and oral rehydration salts, and know that it is important to keep drinking plenty of safe liquids.

PRACTICAL INFORMATION

Banks. The larger towns all have one or more banks as well as exchange offices, and you can usually change money at the hotels and lodges. The banks give standard exchange rates. Street vendors offering to sell *kwachas* for dollars or other currency are best avoided. Most international credit cards are accepted at top-range and mid-range hotels, shops and restaurants, but up-country you cannot depend on local people accepting plastic.

Business hours. Most offices are open Monday to Friday 8 or 9 a.m.–4 or 5 p.m., with an hour for lunch between midday and 2 p.m. Shops are open at roughly the same times from Monday to Saturday.

Climate. The weather is dry and, thanks to the altitude above sea level, quite cool, between May and August. September, October and November tend to be warm and dry, and the warm and steamy rainy season stretches from December to April—since you are south of the Equator, this means the summer months.

Currency. Zambia's currency is the *kwacha* (abbreviated to ZK), issued in notes from 20 to 50,000 ZK. Coins are rarely seen.

Electricity. Mains electricity is 220 volts, delivered at 50 Hz. Most sockets require square British-style three-pin plugs.

Languages. English is the official language, and while many Bantu dialects are spoken locally, it would be rare for English-speaking visitors to have difficulty making themselves understood.

Photography. It is sensible to ask permission before taking close-ups. You are likely to be asked for payment.

Taxis. All taxis carry their number on the door, and can safely be hailed in the street. Always negotiate the fare before boarding.

Time. UTC/GMT + 2 all year round.

Tipping. A standard 10 per cent charge for service is generally added to bills, in which case no tip is, in theory, necessary. The government adds a 23 per cent tax.

Water. Don't drink from (or swim in) rivers! Stick to well-known brands of bottled water or other bottled drinks, and avoid added ice cubes. On safari, all water for drinking should be filtered and purified with readily available purification tablets.

Getting a taste of dad's dinner: a trusting relationship between a lion and his cub.

ON SAFARI

Safari: a journey, in Swahili. Africa is one of the last places in the world to possess wildlife of such rich variety. The countries of Eastern and Southern Africa—especially South Africa, Botswana, Namibia, Zimbabwe, Zambia, Tanzania, Kenya and Uganda—have become world leaders in environmental protection. The size of the protected zones could cover a large part of western Europe.

Mammals

Africa's mammalian fauna embraces more than 1,150 species placed in 13 orders, of which the most diverse are rodents, bats and insectivores. Of greater interest to casual safari-goers, however, is the continent's unique wealth of large mammals—from ferocious carnivores such as lion and leopard to a bewildering profusion of more placid antelopes, from the elephant and rhinoceros to man's closest living relative, the chimpanzee.

Elephant *Loxodonta africana*
The largest animal walking the earth can weigh over 6.5 tonnes, which is perhaps not surprising when you consider that it never stops growing during all of its 80 years. The longest pair of tusks on record measured 3.49 m and weighed 200 kg, but those of an average elephant are around 1 m in length. Heavier and taller than its Asian cousin, the African elephant also has different-shaped ears and trunk. This strange nasal appendage is a magical, multi-purpose tool, extremely flexible thanks to its 500 muscles. It enables the elephant to feed, smell, feel, break off branches, fell trees, lift and carry, shoo flies, and give itself a shower! It also makes an excellent snorkel to help the animal through deep water. They say an elephant never forgets, and it does indeed have a good memory, even though the brain is rather small in proportion to the whole body.

A normal drink for an elephant is about the equivalent of a full bathtub; it downs 10 litres at a time in one gulp. It is always hungry and eats all day long, needing

Claude Hervé-Bazin

istockphoto.com/Omelchenko

Two of the Big Five, elephant and rhinoceros.

and tiny brain, a combination that sees it habitually charging towards anything that moves, including trains, and sometimes things that don't! The **white rhinoceros** *(Ceratotherium simum)*, though significantly bulkier (up to 1,600 kg as opposed to 1,100 kg), is far more placid. Size aside, the main physical difference between black and white rhinos is not the colour but their lip shape—the upper lip of the black rhino forms a pointed hook to clip twigs and leaves, while the white rhino has wide square lips suitable for grazing. It is this—"white" being a mistranslation of the African "weit", meaning wide—that has led to the names white and black rhino.

Rhinoceroses are now locally extinct or headed that way in several reserves that supported populations of several thousand as recently as the 1970s. The main cause of this poaching is the Oriental belief that the horn is a strong aphrodisiac—a legend that might be linked to the animal's lengthy coition, lasting up to an hour. Today, the main stronghold of both species is South Africa, where white and black rhino are protected in significant numbers in the Kruger National Park and various Zululand reserves. The white rhino is almost extinct further north, but isolated populations of black rhino occur in the

about a tenth of its body weight per day to keep going—300 kg of leaves, bark, roots and fruit ground up by the molars (weighing 4 kg each). These are renewed five times during the animal's lifetime, but once the last set has gone, many aged elephants die of hunger as they can no longer feed themselves.

Rhinoceros

The more widespread of Africa's two rhino species, the **black rhinoceros** *(Diceros bicornis)* is known for its bad temper, poor eyesight

Tanzania's Ngorongoro Crater and some private reserves in Kenya.

Hippopotamus
Hippopotamus amphibius
The name literally translates from the Latin as "river horse". Most of the time, pods of a few dozen wade around close to the banks, grunting loudly, but otherwise invisible except for their nostrils and ears poking discreetly above the surface. The nostrils have flaps that close when the animal submerges. The big yawns in which hippos indulge don't mean they are tired: the male opens wide to impress its adversaries with its sharp sickle-like teeth, up to 60 cm in length. Battles between male hippos can be extremely violent and sometimes result in the death of the weaker individual. The hippopotamus normally leaves the water only at night, to graze on the riverbanks—leaving behind piles of droppings to mark its territory.

African buffalo *Syncerus caffer*
A member of the wild ox family, the burly buffalo bulldozes its way through life. All the animals of the savannah, including the normally fearless lion, are wary of it. A wounded buffalo is all the more bad-tempered, and its heavy curved horns can easily rip a victim apart. Most of the time, how-

Claude Hervé-Bazin

Claude Hervé-Bazin

A hippo, the river horse, happy in water and mud. | A burly buffalo.

ever, buffaloes mind their own business, grazing peacefully in herds of up to 2,000 head. The smaller, redder forest buffalo is a West African race whose range extends into parts of Uganda.

Giraffe *Giraffa camelopardalis*
A fully grown giraffe could look through a second-floor window without having to stretch. In the open brush, its 2-m-long neck enables it to reach the leaves of acacia trees, its principal source of food. Its hairy lips and long, prehensile tongue, 40 cm (15 in)

A Rothschild's giraffe enjoying an acacia lunch.

long, act as protection against the acacia's sharp thorns. With such a limited diet, the giraffe has to spend at least 20 hours a day just eating. As it only needs 20 minutes' sleep, it passes most of the time between meals gazing at the landscape (it has excellent eyesight, a wide range of vision and long, flirty eyelashes). On the tip of its tail is a tuft of long hair that is used as a fly swatter. Its neck only has seven cervical vertebra, the same as all other mammals, but each neck bone is greatly elongated—and a strong heart is needed to pump sufficient blood all the way up to the head. To reach anything on the ground, or to drink, the giraffe has to adopt an ungainly posture, spreading its front legs wide.

Several races are recognized. The **southern giraffe** of southern Africa and **Maasai giraffe** of Tanzania and southern Kenya both have a colour pattern of dark blotches on a paler background. The striking **reticulated giraffe** of northern Kenya has quadrangular markings separated by sharply defined narrow white lines. The rare **Rothschild's giraffe**, most easily seen in Kenya's Lake Nakuru National Park, is distinguished by an extra pair of horns, and a lack of spots beneath the knee.

Lion *Panthera leo*
When its roar thunders over the savannah, everything stops. The lion, Africa's largest carnivore, is on the prowl. The main role of the black or golden-maned male lion is to maintain the territory of his pride, a family unit with several generations of females. Hunting is mainly a female activity, and it takes but a second for the lion's great weight and momentum to down a gazelle and break its back, or dispatch it quickly with a bite in the throat. After the kill, the male comes for his share of the meat, chasing the females away. He prefers the innards.

Lioness, the African queen.

hemis.fr/Frances

Despite excellent teamwork, lions do not have a high success rate: four times out of five the prey gets away. Sprawled out beneath a tree, lions generally sleep 20 hours a day. Feverish activity breaks out only when the females are in heat: they can mate up to 80 times daily! It takes their mind off their food. While the females always stay together, the males are chased out after a few years by a rival group. When the dominant male is deposed, the new master of the harem will kill or expel the male cubs of previous litters.

Leopard *Panthera pardus*

The most elusive of Africa's large cats is the leopard, which generally snoozes by day, draped over a high branch hidden by the foliage. At nightfall, when it's

The leopard feels very much at home when up in a tree.

time to start hunting, the perch becomes a lookout. The leopard is quite a gourmet, ready to taste anything from insects to crocodiles, but its main prey consists of baboons or small to medium-sized antelope such as gazelles, which it hauls up to the hideout with the help of strong jaws and 70 kg of muscle.

The leopard's beautiful tan coat is dotted with circular black "rosettes". In certain high-altitude areas such as the Aberdare Mountains, melanistic individuals (panthers) are regularly born into otherwise ordinary litters. Unlike the lion, the leopard is a solitary crea-

istockphoto.com/Johnson

ture; the male stays with the female only during the mating season.

Cheetah *Acinonyx jubatus*

The cheetah is the world's fastest mammal, capable of running at 110 kph (68 mph) to overtake the quickest antelope. A plains dweller, it bursts from the high grass to pursue its prey, but can't maintain high speeds for long and usually gives up an fruitless chase after 500 m. The most diurnal hunter of Africa's large predators, the cheetah has a success rate of 50 percent, twice as good as the lion's. Standing about 1 m (3 ft) tall at the shoulder, and weighing 40–60 kg, the cheetah is easily distinguished from the superficially similar but bulkier leopard by its greyhound build, small round head (with diagnostic black "tear marks" running from eye to mouth) and single as opposed to compound spots. It is the only large feline in the world placed outside the genus Panthera (big cats), due to certain anomalous features such as non-retractable claws. The female gives birth to up to five cubs, but it's rare for more than two to survive beyond 3 months, particularly where densities of rival predators are high.

Serval *Felis serval*

This solitary medium-sized cat is about one-third as bulky as the cheetah and has a similar coat: tawny with rows of black spots along the back. You may catch sight of its pointed, white-patched ears sticking up above high grass. Found in African bush country, the serval feeds on rodents, insects and frogs. A nocturnal animal, it has a novel hunting method that consists of jumping high into the air and letting itself drop onto the unfortunate prey, knocking it out. It can even catch birds in flight.

istockphoto.com/Gombarik

istockphoto.com/Shah

The cheetah: a fast runner. | The sharp-eared serval.

African wildcat *Felis silvestris*

The direct ancestor of the domestic cat, and similar in appearance to a tabby, but with longer legs, the African wild cat is found throughout eastern and southern Africa, but seldom seen as it hunts at night and hides during the day.

Caracal *Caracal caracal*

The caracal is the African equivalent of the lynx: a medium-sized sandy-coloured cat with black facial markings and long-tufted ears. Tolerant of a wide variety of habitats, it is most common in dry rocky savannah, but like the serval it is a secretive nocturnal hunter and seldom observed.

Hyenas

Dog-like in appearance, but more closely related to genets and civets, Africa's four hyena species are all characterized by a sloping back and limping gait. Ubiquitous in most habitats other than desert and rainforest, the **spotted hyena** (*Crocuta crocuta*) is Africa's second bulkiest carnivore, noted for emitting an array of whoops and giggles that resound menacingly through the night. Often portrayed as an

wikimedia.org/Csonka

fotolia.com/Noakes

istockphoto.com/Chamberlain

The elusive wildcat. | **The caracal has distinctive tufted ears.** | **The hyena cleans up other animals' leftovers.**

exclusive scavenger, it actually hunts 60 per cent of its prey. In addition, thanks to a highly developed sense of smell and powerful jaws adapted for crushing bones, it does an excellent job of keeping the landscape clean. The spotted hyena lives in loose clans of 20 to 50 individuals, in which females are dominant over males. In ancient times, the spotted hyena was thought to be hermaphroditic due to the female's unique external genitalia, which consist of a penis-like clitoris and sacs resembling a scrotum.

Scarcer and more localized, the handsome **striped hyena** *(Hyaena hyaena),* with its distinctive black-and-cream striped coat and long shaggy spinal crest, is a northern species whose range extends into drier parts of Kenya and Tanzania. The **brown hyena** *(Hyaena brunnea),* restricted to Botswana, Namibia and bordering regions of Zimbabwe and South Africa, can be recognized by its lustrous brown coat and cream neck cape.

The **aardwolf** *(Proteles cristata),* an elusive resident of semi-arid country, superficially resembles a miniature striped hyena, but feeds almost exclusively on harvester termites.

The wild dog hunts in packs, preying on mammals but also large birds.

African wild dog *Lycaon pictus*

Also known as the hunting or painted dog, Africa's largest canid has rounded ears, long legs, black skin and a sparse, mottled fur of black, yellow and white. Highly sociable, it lives and travels in packs of up to 50 individuals, with a majority of males. Within packs, usually only one couple does all the breeding. Of all African animals, it is the best hunter and incredibly ferocious, hunting in relays, which obstinately pursue their prey until it collapses exhausted. Persecuted in some areas and eliminated by rabies elsewhere, the wild dog is highly endangered, with an estimated 5,000 remaining in the wild. The most important stronghold is the vast Selous Game Reserve, with at least 1,000 individuals. Wild dogs are quite common in the Kruger National Park.

Jackals *Canis spp*

Placed in the same genus as domestic dogs—which they

Didier Nicolet

resemble in appearance and behaviourally—two species of jackal are widely distributed in eastern and southern Africa. The **black-backed jackal** (*C. mesomelas*) is associated with acacia habitats, and is more common than the **side-striped jackal** (*C. adustus*) except in the miombo woodland belt of Zimbabwe, Zambia and southern Tanzania. Both species are fawn-brown with a silvery-black back, but wide regional variation in coloration means that the most reliable way to tell them apart is by the colour of the tail tip—white in the side-striped but black in the black-backed. The **common** (or Eurasian) **jackal** (*C. aureus*) is a northern species whose range extends south to central Tanzania: all three species cohabit the Serengeti-Ngorongoro ecosystem in northern Tanzania. Jackals are opportunistic omnivores, feeding on anything from carrion, freshly hunted birds and mammals, and fruits and bulbs. Their soul-searching musical howl, a love call, is a characteristic sound of the African night.

Bat-eared fox
Otocyon megalotis
Associated with dry acacia savannah, the bat-eared fox is an endearing small canid with a thick grey-red coat, large ears and a distinctive black "robber's

Black-backed jackal. | **A close-knit family of bat-eared foxes.**

mask" around the eyes. Generally seen in pairs, sometimes with off-spring in tow, it is particularly visible in Tanzania's Serengeti and the Kgalagadi Transfrontier Park.

Zebra *Equus spp*
To human observers, the distinctive black-and-white striped coat of the zebra may seem to defeat the purpose, but this camouflage system does work very well in the bush. Blurred by the heat haze, the mingled silhouettes of the herd create a dazzling optical

Ariadne van Zandbergen

A zebra's striping pattern is unique to each individual.

ized by light brown "shadows" between the black stripes. The endangered **Grévy's zebra** (*E. grevyi*), almost twice as bulky and more narrowly striped, is restricted to arid plains in northern Kenya and Ethiopia. Two races of **mountain zebra** (*E. zebra*) are endemic respectively to South Africa and Namibia, where they can be distinguished from local races of plains zebra by the absence of shadow stripes. The **Cape mountain zebra** (*E. z. zebra*) is an endangered fynbos inhabitant of the southern Cape, where fewer than 1000 surviving individuals are protected in various provincial reserves. An estimated 7,000 **Hartmann's mountain zebra** (*E. z. hartmannae*) survive in the arid coastal belt of Namibia.

Blue wildebeest
Connochaetes taurinus

With horns like handlebars and a cow's head, a skinny body, bushy beard and long fly-swatter tail, the wildebeest (or gnu, as the Hottentots say) resembles an African version of the bison. In summer, the mass migration of hundreds of thousands of white-bearded wildebeest, crossing the plains of East Africa in search of fresh grass, makes an impressive spectacle. It braves every danger: attacks by big cats, crocodile-infested rivers, and the birth of calves along the way.

illusion that completely throws predators. It confuses the lions, and is even thought to spoil the aim of pesky insects. A gregarious animal, the zebra shares its territory with wildebeest and antelopes. It lives in herds numbering several dozen, and during the migratory season can travel in groups of a thousand or more.

Three species of zebra are recognized. The widespread **plains zebra** (*E. quagga*) is a common savannah resident throughout eastern and southern Africa, with the more southerly races character-

Claude Hervé-Bazin

In South Africa, the local sub-species of blue wildebeest has a black beard.

Black wildebeest
Connochaetes gnou
Endemic to the grassy South African highveld and Swaziland, this formerly common antelope —darker than the blue wildebeest and with a distinctive white tail— was reduced by hunting to an estimated 4,000 individuals, but the numbers have risen to 10,000, many protected on private ranches. A good place to look for it is Golden Gate National Park.

Hartebeest
Alcelaphus buselaphus
Found in fairly large herds on the grassy savannah and plains of East Africa, where it frequently accompanies zebras and wildebeest on their migration, this ani-

The black wildebeest or white-tailed gnu; Coke's hartebeest is also known as the kongoni.

mal is easily identified by its stately air, its exceptionally long face, and its shiny coat. Seven races are recognized, each with a distinctive horn shape. Most common in East Africa is **Coke's hartebeest**, sandy in colour and with widespread lyre-shaped horns mounted on bony pedestals covered with hair. **Lichtenstein's hartebeest** (southern Tanzania and Zambia) is regarded by some authorities as a full species, with horns that close together like a scorpion's pincers. Those of the tawny **Jackson's hartebeest** are somewhere between the two, forming a U-shape. The **red harte-**

wikimedia.org/Vassil

istockphoto.com/Trolle

Two friendly topi and a blesbok.

Bontebok *Damaliscus pygargus*
Endemic to South Africa, this lightly built relation of the topi was hunted close to extinction in the 19th century and most of the extant population is domestic. Two very distinct races occur: the **blesbok** *(D. p. phillipsi)* of the highveld has a white blaze on the forehead and greenish-yellow horns, while the **bontebok** *(D. p. pygargus)* of the Cape fynbos has a white tail and "socks". A good place to see them is the Bontebok National Park near Swellendam.

Common eland
Taurotragus oryx
With a shoulder height of up to 1.8 m (6 ft), the common eland is heavier even than the massive buffalo. It has heavy folds of skin hanging from the neck and spirally twisting horns. Despite its weight, it can gallop as fast as a horse and make quite impressive jumps. Its hair is short and fawn-coloured, with vertical white lines behind the hump on its back.

beest of southern Africa has a paler, rustier coloration than the more northerly races.

Topi *Damaliscus lunatus*
Known as the tsessebe in southern Africa, the topi is closely related to the hartebeest and similar in overall appearance, but much darker. Common on the grassy plains of East Africa, it is usually seen in small family groups, but occasionally travels in herds of several hundred.

Eland, the world's largest antelope.

Greater kudu
Tragelaphus strepsiceros
The second-largest African antelope, the stately greater kudu, is common in southern Africa, but scarce further north, having been all but eliminated by rinderpest in the 1890s. The male has magnificent corkscrew horns that can reach 1 m in length. The coat is light brown, bluish grey down the sides with narrow white bands. It has a long tuft of hair hanging from the throat. It typically lives in herds of 5–10 individuals, with the sexes mingling only in the breeding season, when the males clash in thundering duels.

Lesser kudu
Tragelaphus imberbis
Absent from southern Africa, the lesser kudu looks similar to the greater kudu, but is smaller, darker and marked with extra stripes — including a white arrow between the eyes. Generally timid, small herds are most likely to be seem in semi-arid reserves such as Ruaha National Park (Tanzania) and Samburu National Reserve (Kenya).

Bushbuck *Tragelaphus scriptus*
Widespread and common, the bushbuck is a rather shy and solitary inhabitant of thicket and forest. It is a very handsome creature, with a dark chestnut coat, a "harness" of two horizontal white stripes on the flanks, and half a dozen vertical stripes on each side. The male has short, stream-

Photodisc Collection

Kudu male and female; both have vertical stripes on the body.

Ariadne van Zandbergen

Ariadne van Zandbergen

Bernard Joliat

The bushbuck is shy and rarely seen. | The nyala has a shaggy coat.

lined, spiralling horns which help it to force its way through the bush.

Nyala *Tragelaphus angasii*
Restricted to the eastern lowveld of southern Africa, the nyala is quite common within its limited range, particularly in northern KwaZulu Natal. The male, slate grey in colour, has a splendid fringe of brown hair on the throat

The sitatunga can hide underwater from its predators.

and under the belly, in addition to a long white mane from shoulder to tail. The female is smaller and reddish brown, with sharply defined white stripes. Only the males have horns, which are lyre-shaped and seem particularly threatening to adversaries in the combats that take place in the rutting season.

Sitatunga
Tragelaphus spekei
The swamp-dwelling sitatunga, also called marshbuck, has very long, slender hooves and spreading toes which help it move over soft mud. In case of danger, it dives underwater and swims away. The fur is soft and brown, lighter in the female, with white stripes and dots on the sides. Although widespread, the sitatunga is often elusive due to the inaccessibility of its favoured habitat. Reliable sites include Rubondo Island (Tanzania), Saiwa Swamp (Kenya) and the Okavango Delta (Botswana).

istockphoto.com/Zejdl

Bongo *Tragelaphus eurycerus*

The bongo is a large forest ante-lope with a rich chestnut coat, a dozen vertical white stripes on the body, a white band from eye to eye, and a short, stubby mane. Both sexes have horns. A critically endangered species, it is represented in East Africa by an isolated population in Kenya's Aberdare National Park, but since 2004 efforts have been made to re-introduce to Mount Kenya a group of animals bred in captivity in North American zoos; their offspring will be released into the wild.

Reedbuck *Redunca spp*

Three species of reedbuck are recognized: **bohor** (*R. redunca*), **southern** (*R. arundinum*) and **mountain** (*R. fulvorufala*). All are slender, light brown, and stand about 75 cm (30 in) tall at the shoulder. The bohor and southern reedbuck frequent marshes and grassland near water, with the former essentially restricted to eastern Africa and the latter to southern Africa, though their ranges overlap in Tanzania. The mountain reedbuck has a prominent patch of naked skin beneath the ear—a scent gland for marking its territory.

Female bongo. | The mountain reed-buck lives in thick forest.

Waterbuck
Kobus ellipsiprymnus

The waterbuck is a powerful animal, dark brown in colour and defensive of its territory. The male sports a pair of long, ridged horns that form a graceful U-shape. It lives near lakes, water-holes and rivers and is a good swimmer, taking refuge in the water when pursued.

Two distinctive races of water-buck exist. The **common waterbuck** (southern Africa and East Africa east of the Rift Valley) is greyish in colour and has prominent white crescents on its rump, while the **Defassa waterbuck** (East

flickr.com/Mara 1

wikimedia.org/Hof

Claude Hervé-Bazin

Ariadne van Zandbergen

Africa west of the Rift Valley) has a more rufous coat and a full white rump.

Sable antilope
Hippotragus niger
Localized and elusive, the sable is a remarkably elegant antelope, in particular the male, with its black coat, contrasting white belly and snout, and sickle-shaped horns that grow to 1.5 m long. The sable inhabits miombo woodland in southern Tanzania, Zambia and Zimbabwe, where the largest population—as high as 30,000—is protected within the Selous Game Reserve. It is common near Pretoriuskop in the Kruger National Park, and an isolated population is easily observed in Shimba Hills National Reserve (Kenya).

Roan antilope
Hippotragus equinus
Similar in appearance to the smaller but more spectacularly horned sable, the roan has a greyish-brown coat offset by a black and white face. The males are extremely aggressive and engage in bloody battles during the rutting season. Present in the miombo woodland of Zambia,

The waterbuck has a white bib a round its throat. | Female sable antelopes can have chestnut coats.

Roan antelope live in harems with one dominant male.

Zimbabwe and Angola, the roan is also common in Tanzania's Ruaha National Park and the northern Kruger National Park.

Oryx *Oryx gazella*

Equine in build and sandy grey in colour, the oryx has black markings on its face and forelegs and a triangular head with straight horns. Three geographically isolated races—regarded by some authorities as full species—live in hot dry climates, where they can survive for long periods without water. The **beisa oryx** (*O. g. beisa*) has long, straight horns and is confined to northeast Kenya and Ethiopia. The **fringe-eared oryx** (*O. g. callotis*) has little tufts of hair on the points of its ears, and is restricted to southeast Kenya and northern Tanzania. A common resident of drier parts of southern Africa, the **gemsbok** (*O. g. gazella*) has rapier-like horns that curve slightly backwards and are used for fighting.

Impala *Aepyceros melampus*

Another acacia-eater, the impala has a definite spring in its step: it can clear 10 m in length and 3 m in height with no problem at all. When danger threatens, the whole herd starts jumping around in apparent disorder, thoroughly confusing the predators. The male, beneath its handsome pair of lyre-shaped horns, lords it over a harem of up to 100 females.

The oryx can kill lions with its powerful horns. | A graceful male impala.

Superficially similar to gazelles, but more closely related to wildebeest and hartebeest, the impala can be easily recognized by its long neck, triangular head and three black stripes on the tail and hindquarters; if any doubt subsists, look at the rear hooves, which are fetchingly fringed by a tuft of black hairs. Arguably the most successful antelope species, the impala is abundant in most acacia habitats in eastern and southern Africa.

Grant's gazelle *Nanger granti*
In proportion to its body, Grant's gazelle has the longest horns of all the antelopes: those of the male can measure as much as 70 cm for a shoulder height of 1 m. A graceful beast, admired for its big dark eyes, it lives in large herds in the plains and grasslands of East Africa. It can be distinguished from Thomson's gazelle by its white tail. Its hindquarters, also white, are marked by vertical black stripes.

Claude Hervé-Bazin

Thomson's Gazelle is a very sociable creature.

Thomson's gazelle
Eudorcas thomsoni
Slender and elegant, Thomson's gazelle has two wide black bands diagonally crossing its flanks. The hindquarters are also white, outlined in black. The tail, perpetually in movement, is dark. During the dry season, the gazelles collect in herds of thousands on the plains of East Arica.

Springbok
Antidorcas marsupialis
South Africa's national animal—and the only gazelle found in southern Africa—looks very similar to Thomson's gazelle, with the same coat, the same black side-band, and the same dark stripe on the sides of its face. However, its tail is white and its horns are finer. A white patch on

istockphoto.com/Gibson

Grant's gazelle adapts well to semi-arid conditions.

the hindquarters contains scent glands. Capable of overtaking a moving vehicle, the springbok shows off its strength by jumping and arching its back, lifting the white hairs under its tail—a behaviour called pronking.

Claude Hervé-Bazin

Gerenuk *Litocranius walleri*

With its interminable, slender neck, the gerenuk can stretch higher than most other antelopes to reach the acacia leaves and twigs that form its diet. It often stands on its long hind legs to nibble as far up the tree as possible. It lives in arid regions and can go without water for long periods. Its fur is dark beige and its horns rather short. Absent from southern Africa, it is widely distributed in arid parts of East Africa, in particular Samburu National Reserve and Tsavo East.

WWF/Harvey

Duikers

Duikers are small secretive forest antelope characterized by sloping backs and richly coloured coats. Most of the 18 recognized species are confined to West Africa, but the **blue duiker** *(Cephalophus monticola)* is common in the forests of the eastern coastal belt, as are the **red duiker** *(C. natalensis)* and

The springbok pronks to ward off predators or attract a mate. | The gerenuk, adept at stretching. | Red duiker.

AfriPics.com/Stanton

Ariadne van Zandbergen

wikimedia.org/Rooivalk

Ulrich Ackermann

Harvey's duiker *(C. harveyi)*, south and north of the Tanzania-Mozambique border respectively. The endangered **Ader's duiker** *(C. adersi)*, endemic to coastal woodland in East Africa, is virtually extinct except on Zanzibar Island. The larger **Abbott's duiker** *(C. spadix)* is confined to a few montane forests in Tanzania. The **common duiker** *(Sylvicapra grimmia)*, the only savannah dwelling duiker, is locally very common.

Other small antelope

As many as a dozen small antelope species occur eastern and southern Africa. One of the most distinctive is the **klipspringer** *(Oreotragus oreotragus)*, an agile resident of rocky hills, some 50 cm high at the shoulder, with a grizzled yellowish-brown coat, long ears, and short spiked horns. The **oribi** *(Ourebia ourebi)* is about the same size as the klipspringer, but lives in tall grassland, and has a light tan coat, black tail tip, and diagnostic black scent gland behind the eye. Smaller than the above is **Kirk's dikdik** *(Madoqua kirkii)*, a savannah and thicket species, with small, straight horns projecting backwards, bold white eye rings, and an unusual protruding nose.

Three small antelope: klipspringer, oribi and dikdik.

istockphoto.com/Trolle

Warthogs are shortsighted but have a good sense of smell.

Warthog
(Phacochoerus aethiopicus)
The warthog is a widespread savannah resident named for the large warts that grow on each side of its long, flat face. It has a bristly mane, long tusks, and a rather comic habit of running off with its tail raised stiffly in the air. Largely diurnal, the warthog is often seen in small family groups, in a characteristic kneeling position, snuffling around for roots and insects.

Hyraxes
Although they look like overgrown rats, hyraxes are more closely related to elephants than to rodents. The **rock hyrax** *(Procavia capensis),* a sociable vegetarian associated with rocky outcrops, is

The hyrax is fat and furry, with a short tail. | Civets were long kept in captivity for their musk.

capable of ascending near-vertical rocks thanks to its friction-padded feet. The nocturnal **tree hyrax** *(Dendrohyrax arboreus)* almost never comes down to the ground, and emits an utterly spine-chilling shrieking cry.

Civet *Civettictis civetta*
In the 17th century, the civet was still found in Europe, where its musk—squirted out defensively into an enemy's face or to scent its territory—was used in the perfume industry as a fixative. The African civet has a long heavy torso marked with black and tan spots and stripes, and a pointed

Claude Hervé-Bazin

BIOS/Seitre

weasel-like muzzle. Seldom observed by day, it is often seen sniffing along the ground on night drives. Although predominantly carnivorous, it also feeds on fruits.

Genets *Genetta spp*

This genus of roughly 10 small nocturnal carnivore species is distinguished from the closely related civet by a more streamlined appearance, relatively lightly spotted coat and long slinky black-ringed tail. Genets also differ from civets in having retractable claws, allowing them to climb trees with ease. To hunt, the genet slinks stealthily through the grass before pouncing on its prey; it seems to kill partly for pleasure as it never finishes all of its meal. The two most common species are the **small-spotted genet** (*G. genetta*) and **large-spotted genet** (*G. tigrina*), which can be differentiated by their tail tips — respectively cream and black. Among the most beautiful and graceful of African predators, genets are very habituated at some lodges, where they wander fearlessly through the dining room.

Mongoose

The 23 species of African mongoose have in common a pup-like face with small eyes and ears, a slender body, relatively uniform coloration, and strongly terrestrial habits. Contrary to legend, no African mongoose feeds mainly on snakes — insects, rodents, lizards, carrion, crustaceans and even fruits form the core diet of various species. Most African mongooses are solitary and nocturnal, including the large **white-tailed mongoose** (*Ichneumia albicauda*), which is often observed on night drives in savannah habitats. The two species most likely to be seen on safari are both highly sociable and mainly diurnal. These are the **banded mongoose** (*Mungos mungo*), distinguished by its faintly striped grizzled grey coat, and the **dwarf mongoose** (*Helogale parvula*), often seen poking their heads inquisitively from burrow entrances in a termite mound. The most socially sophisticated mongoose is the **suricate** or meerkat (*Suricata suricata*), a denizen of the arid western half

BIOS/Ransom

Like civets, genets have strong musk glands.

Mongoose, constantly on the alert.

of southern Africa. The main group will sit together on their haunches, while a sentry is posted on the nearest vantage point to raise the alarm when an intruder enters their territory — at which point the whole group scurries off into the safety of its subterranean burrow network.

Aardvark *Orycteropus afer*

Placed in a unique order, this amazing insectivore combines characteristics of many other animals: a vaguely pig-like snout and feet, long rabbit-like ears, and a body and tail something like the kangaroo. Nocturnal and solitary, the aardvark breaks open termite nests with its claws and captures the insects with its long, sticky tongue. It can fight but usually, when attacked, it will hastily dig out a burrow.

Both aardvarks and pangolins feed on ants and termites.

Pangolin *Manis spp*

Shy and timorous, the pangolin, or scaly anteater, is clad in a coat of mail strong enough to withstand all attacks. When threatened, it rolls up into a tight ball like a hedgehog and lifts its scales towards the aggressor. These are so sharp they can scratch metal! A nocturnal animal, the pangolin feeds on termites and ants, catching them with its exceedingly long, sticky tongue. It is toothless, but can tear apart termite nests with its front claws. The largest of the four African pangolins, *M. gigantea,* can measure 1.5 m (5 ft) in length.

A chimpanzee ready for a comfortable nap. | Baboons are ground-dwellers but also climb trees.

Chimpanzee *Pan troglodytes*

Man's closest living relative is a rainforest species whose range extends as far east as Lake Tanganyika in western Tanzania. Chimpanzees live in extended communities of up to 150 individuals, and their home territories are fiercely protected by the males, which—unlike the more mobile females—seldom leave the community into which they were born. Tanzania's population of 2,000 wild chimpanzees represents 1 per cent of the continental total, but it's well protected and has been the subject of extensive research, most famously by Jane Goodall in Gombe Stream. Here, and in the Mahale Mountains National Park, habituated chimps can be approached within metres on guided foot excursions.

Africa's other two great ape species, the bonobo and gorilla, are absent from southern Africa, Kenya and Tanzania, but habituated gorilla troops can be visited in Uganda.

Baboon *Papio papio*

The size of a large dog, with a long, canine face and fearsome jaw, the baboon is a gregarious animal, living in troops of up to 100 members, under the authority of a dominant male. If the ruler takes priority for food and delousing, it does not enjoy the privileges of a harem, for when the females are in heat they offer themselves to any available partner. Powerful and aggressive, baboons are common residents of savannah habitats throughout eastern and southern Africa, but are most prolific in open, rocky territory and avoid forests. Three races—regarded by many authorities as full species—are found in the region. The **olive baboon** *(P. p. anubis),* which occurs in East Africa west of the Rift Valley, is the bulkiest and most imposing, weighing up to 50 kg and also with a prominent cape. The paler and more lightly built **yellow baboon** *(P. p. cynocephalus)* ranges east of the Rift Valley, and is replaced by the dark grey **chacma baboon** *(P. p. ursinus)* in southern Africa.

Forest guenons
Cercopithecus spp

The guenons of the genus Cercopithecus are mostly forest monkeys of West/Central Africa, the most notable exception being the **Sykes monkey** *(C. albogularis),* a localized resident of riverine and other forests in eastern and southern Africa. The **red-tailed monkey** *(C. ascanius),* easily recognized by its bold white nose patch, occurs in forested habitats in southwestern Kenya and around Lake Tanganyika. **De Brazza's monkey** *(C. neglectus),* distinguished by its striking white beard, is resident in Kenya's Saiwa Swamp National Park.

Another member of the Cercopithecus family, the **vervet monkey** *(Chlorocebus pygerythrus)* can be recognized by its grizzled grey coat, black face, fringe of long white hairs, and the male's bright blue scrotum. An adaptable and opportunistic omnivore, it is an unusually terrestrial monkey, and troops of 20 or more are ubiquitous except in deserts and forest interiors. Habituated vervet monkeys often live in the vicinity of lodges, making frequent raids on the buffet table.

Ariadne van Zandbergen

Ariadne van Zandbergen

Claude Hervé-Bazin

The Cercopithecidae are "Old World" monkeys: Sykes or white-throated, red-tailed, and vervet.

Ariadne van Zandbergen

Photodisc Collection

Patas are fast runners. | **Black and white colobus, or mantled guereza.**

Patas monkey
Erythrocebus patas
Like the baboon and vervet, the patas is a terrestrial monkey, but it has a spindlier build, a reddish coat and a black stripe above the eyes. Its core range is the dry savannah of the Sahel, extending into the northwest of Kenya, but an isolated population lives in Tanzania's Serengeti National Park.

Colobus monkeys
The colobus monkeys are medium-sized, thumbless forest-dwellers that subsist largely on leaves and live in troops of 10 to several hundred individuals. Absent from southern Africa, they are well represented in East Africa, in particular the spectacular **black and white colobus** *(Colobus guereza),* which occurs in most montane and some lowland forests.

The Central African **red colobus** *(Piliocolobus oustaleti)* is a Congolese species whose range extends into Gombe Stream and Mahale Mountains National Parks, where it is regularly hunted by chimpanzees.

Three red colobus species endemic to East Africa are listed as endangered by the IUCN, none boasting populations of greater than 2,000. **Kirk's red colobus** *(P. kirkii),* notable for its unkempt white fringe, is unique to Zanzibar, and is readily approached in Jozani Forest Reserve. The **Iringa red colobus** *(P. gordonorum)* and **Tana River red colobus** *(P. rufomitratus)* are respectively confined to the Udzungwa Mountains (Tanzania) and the Tana River (Kenya).

Bushbabies
Bushbabies are primitive nocturnal primates, closely related to the lemurs of Madagascar, with soft woolly fur, large round eyes and a tail longer than the body. Several species are recognized, of

which the largest is the rabbit-sized **greater galago** *(Otolemur crassicaudatus)*. You may see one leaping from branch to branch on a night drive, but are more likely to hear its piercing scream—a special rallying call.

Reptiles

Southern Africa can boast more than 400 species of reptile–cold-blooded, scaly animals–including 130 species of snake.

Nile crocodile
Crocodilus niloticus
The crocodile haunts most African rivers and lakes, and is often seen during the hottest hours of the day sunning on a sandbank. In the water, only its protruding nostrils, its eyes and part of the back are visible, like floating pieces of driftwood. The reptile lunges onto its prey and drags it thrashing underwater to drown, then leaves the body to tenderize beneath a rock or immersed tree trunk for a few days, since its teeth are not sharp enough to tear up fresh meat. A crocodile can go for six months without eating and lives up to 70 years. It lays eggs in the sand or mud of the river banks, which incubate for three months. The hatchlings measure 15 cm (6 in) at birth, growing into adults 6 m (20 ft) long.

BIOS/Thouvenin

istockphoto.com/5mit

The bushbaby sleeps in a nest of leaves or a hole in a tree. | A crocodile has 64 to 70 teeth.

Chameleon *Chamaeleo*
As fast as lightening, the chameleon's tongue—as long as its body—shoots out, stuns the victim and glues it up. A fraction of a second later, the dreaded weapon is back in place, folded like an accordion at the back of the throat. With special 3-D vision, the chameleon can judge distances with precision; its eyes move independently, enabling it to see what's going on in front and behind. Contrary to legend, chameleons do not change colour

A camouflage artist. | The rock python.

for camouflage, but in response to their mood. Most species are green or brown in their normal state, but turn red or black when angry and white in the absence of light. Among the most striking of the 140 African species are those with horns, used in combat.

Snakes

Possibly the most feared of all vertebrates, snakes are abundant in Africa, but thankfully also very timid and secretive, and unlikely to be encountered unless actively searched for. Most snakes are non-venomous, and fatal bites are rare (in South Africa, lightning accounts for a greater number of deaths than snakebites!), but it is wise to wear heavy boots and long trousers when walking in the bush as a precaution.

The largest African snake—up to 7 m long—is the **rock python** *(Python sebae)* which feeds on small mammals it strangles to death.

Lizards

More conspicuous than snakes, Africa's lizards range in size from pinkie-length skinks to the 2-m long water monitor. One of the most familiar African lizards, often resident in hotel rooms, where it snaffles up insects attracted to the lights, is the house gecko, which is somewhat spectral in appearance due its almost transparent white skin, and has feet so adhesive it can run upside-

The gecko is a welcome guest as it eats mosquitoes and other insects.

down on a smooth ceiling. The agama family of garishly coloured lizards—blue, orange, purple and pink—is often associated with rocky habitats.

Birds

Kenya and Tanzania alone each boast in excess of 1,000 bird species and more than 1,700 have been recorded in eastern and southern Africa as a whole. Some of the more common and conspicuous savannah species are described below.

Ostrich *Struthio camelus*
Too bulky to fly, the ostrich has adapted to earthbound conditions by learning to run. With its long powerful legs, it can reach a speed of 70 kph (43 mph). The full-grown male is about 2.4 m (8 ft) tall and weighs 140 kg. The ostrich lives in small groups dominated by one, polygamous male, with black plumage and white wings and tail feathers. The females are greyish-brown. They all lay eggs in the same nest, a large depression in the sand; there may be 40 eggs altogether, each weighing 2 kg! It's often said that the ostrich will eat anything. In fact, its diet consists of grass, fruit, insects and small mammals. It does, however, swallow a large quantity of sand. merely for digestive purposes.

Ostrich family outing. | Fish eagle spying on river fish from its perch.

Fish eagle *Haliaetus vocifer*
The most striking of more than a dozen African eagle species, the fish eagle is a familiar sight around the lakes and rivers, perched on its nest or on the topmost branches of a tall tree. It is easily recognized by its plumage: all the top of its body—head, neck and breast—is white, and the rest a brownish-black. It feeds mainly on fish, which it skilfully skims from the lake surface and carries back to its perch, or on young flamingos, leaving only a nasty mess of pink feathers.

istockphoto.com/Icarusimages

istockphoto.com/Gijsbers

Two bald-headed scavengers, the vulture and the marabou stork.

istockphoto.com/Yu

Claude Hervé-Bazin

Vultures

Among the more common of nine vulture species found in Africa are the **hooded vulture** (*Necrosyrtes monachus*) and the **white backed vulture** (*Gryps africanus*). Most have similar features: an S-shaped neck, unfeathered head, large, hooked beak. And all vultures feed on carrion, which they spy from afar as they glide tirelessly over the savannah, taking advantage of rising thermals to stay high in the air without having to waste any effort. However, they are not very good at lifting off from the ground. Sometimes, when the bird has over-eaten (its gizzard can hold 6 kg of food), it just has to give up!

Marabou stork
Leptoptilos crumeniferus

Bald, with a large, inflatable sack hanging from the base of its pink neck, the marabou stork is one of the ugliest birds in existence. It uses its long, strong beak to tear strips of flesh from decaying corpses. Its taste for carrion — or anything else of animal origin — has encouraged it to come closer to the towns where it feeds in rubbish tips. Like the other storks, the marabou is dumb: to make a noise it snaps its beak.

Secretary bird
Sagittarius serpentarius

Despite its long, thin legs, the bluish-grey secretary bird is a raptor, more closely related to eagles than to storks or cranes. It seldom flies and is solitary, building nests of twigs in trees or bushes. It's often said that the name comes from its crest of feathers that look like quill pens stuck behind a clerk's ear, but in fact it is simply a mispronunciation of the Arabic name for the species. A fast runner, the bird preys on reptiles, especially snakes, stalking them through the grass and stunning them with its powerful, hooked beak and feet.

The secretary bird helps control the snake population.

Crowned crane
Balearica regulorum

With dark grey plumage and a golden fan-shaped crest, the crowned crane is one of the most handsome birds in Africa. It lives in pairs or small flocks near swamps, on lake shores and in grasslands. During the breeding season, they can be seen performing fascinating nuptial dances: face to face, the birds spread their wings, lift off suddenly into the air and let themselves fall, chase around on the ground and then start all over again.

Flamingos

The **Greater flamingo** (*Phoenicopterus ruber*) is also found in the Mediterranean and the Caribbean, being twice as big as the **Lesser flamingo** (*P. minor*), by far the most abundant species. On the alkaline lakes of the East African Rift, the colonies can number up to 2 million birds, a spectacular sight. They feed on shrimp and microscopic algae, which give their feathers a pink tinge—dipping their heads under the water and scooping backwards with the head upside down. The bill is equipped with a filter that retains the food and strains out the water. The bird often stands on one leg, with the other tucked under the body—perhaps a way to retain body heat though no one is quite sure.

The crowned crane certainly has a regal bearing. | Lesser or greater, the flamingo is always stunning.

Hornbills *Bucerotidae*

These mostly black-and-white birds have large, curved beaks and some unusual habits. When nesting, the female walls herself up into the hollow of a tree, plastering over the entrance with mud which the male brings in pellets. Only a small slit is left for the male to pass in food. Once the eggs have hatched, the male provides for the whole family until the female can leave the nest. The chicks reseal the entrance and both parents continue to feed them until they are big enough to fend for themselves. The **grey** (*Tockus nasutus*), **yellow-billed** (*T. leucomelas*) and **red-billed** (*T. erythrorhynchus*) hornbills, widespread in savannah habitats, are moderately large birds—about the size of a magpie—but the Tockus are dwarfed by forest species of hornbills such as the **trumpeter** (*Bycanistes bucinator*), which as its name suggests is also exceptionally noisy. More impressive still is the **ground hornbill** (*Bucorvus leadbeateri*), a largely terrestrial savannah species that is about the size of a large turkey. It is the only hornbill that does not seal up its nest.

Weavers *Ploceus spp*

Africa's many species of seed-eating weaver birds are members of the passerine family. The males are generally brightly coloured, red or yellow and black. Using grass, leaf-fibres or twigs, they weave their home according to a precise, complicated plan. The entry is almost always at the bottom, facing downwards.

The species known as the **Sociable weaver** (*Philetairus socius*) builds round or bottle-shaped nests fixed to branches; one tree colony can consist of dozens of nests inhabited by up to 400 tenants, like an enormous apartment complex.

istockphoto.com/Richter

flickr.com/Evans

Yellow-billed hornbill. | **Weaver at work on its beautiful nest.**

General editor
Barbara Ender-Jones

Revision
Philip Briggs

Design
Karin Palazzolo

Layout
Luc Malherbe
Matias Jolliet

Photo credits
P. 1: istockphoto.com/Dopplmayr
P. 2: istockphoto.com/Lamb (basket); /Badenhorst (vineyard); flickr.com/flowcomm (lion)
Ariadne van Zandbergen (girl with bead necklace)

Maps
JPM Publications, Mathieu Germay

JPM Publications S.A.
12, avenue William-Fraisse,
1006 Lausanne, Switzerland
information@jpmguides.com
http://www.jpmguides.com/

Printed in Germany
14321.00.8546
Edition 2011

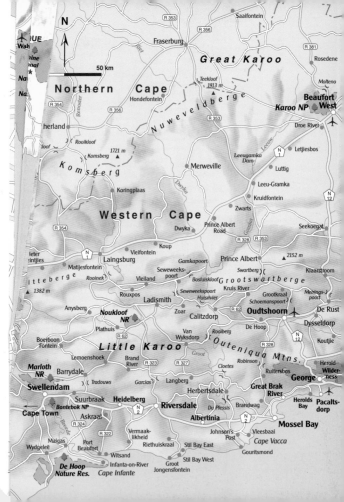

Garden Route and the South